Educational guidelines by the Hitler Youth

Service in the Jungmädelbund
Guidelines
For the first year of service

Educational guideline by the Hitler Youth

Service in the Jungmädelbund

Guidelines
for the
first year of service

Issued by the Reichs Youth Leadership

Berlin, the 1. February 1940

With the issuing of this educational guideline for the service for the First year of the Jungmädelbund in the Hitler Youth, all previous rules and regulations are declared obsolete.

Compilation and editing: Organization office of the RJF

Distributor: JM5

O.-No. II/40-65 000. Questions are to be directed to the

Office for organization Reichs Youth Leadership,

Berlin W35, Kurfürstenstraße 53.

Print: Rotadruck Wilhelm Meyer KG, Berlin SW

Originally published as:
Ausbildungsvorschrift der Hitler-Jugend
Der Dienst im Jungmädelbund in der Hitler-Jugend
Richtlinien für Dienst des ersten Jahrganges - 1940

English Translation by Vera Filthaut and Cynthia A. Sandor

BDM History Publishing
149 Garden St.
Conneaut, Ohio 44030
417-597-3083
https://bdmhistory.com

ISBN# 979-8985456721 – Hardback
ISBN# 979-8985456738 – Paperback
ISBN# 979-8985456745 – E-book

In Loving Memory of

Vera Filthaut

The Youth Leader of the German Reich:

The youth are enriched less by the experience of the older generation, than by the necessary errors through which they

alone come to their own experience. Only this is life. One can only become wise through oneself, never through others. The border between knowledge and education is drawn where a young person seeks adventure. Sober knowledge, knowledge of materials, and numbers can be taught. But, to educate youth requires a brave heart. What are the basic elements of the education we require? They are those virtues that, at the same time, dictate the German nature: Reverence, loyalty and sacrifice.

Baldur von Schirach

Reichs Leader

Contents

Preface

Jungmädel leader! With the law issued on 1 December 1936 the Führer has given us a beautiful task: to educate in addition to home and school, all boys and girls in the Hitler Youth from the age of 10 onwards to be responsible Germans.

We are proud that our Jungmädel service forms the beginning of the great aim to educate all German girls in the spirit of National Socialism, in order to serve our nation.

But we are also aware, that this goal can only be achieved, if in the first four years of this educational community, the Jungmädelbund nurtures our girls, who of course are all comrades who fulfil all the requirements of their little community happily and with a sense of duty, who are all healthy, fresh, brave and loyal. Those are the Jungmädel we want to hand over to the BDM, and this is only possible if our Jungmädel leaders conduct planned and carefully thought-out work right from the onset which in turn will enable the Jungmädel to naturally progress into larger and greater tasks.

Our entire young girls' work is structured and builds up organically. This is necessary because one cannot expect from a ten-year-old girl what we would expect from a twelve- to thirteen-year-old. This training regulation will provide you with the material for the first year, further training regulations will be published for the subsequent years.

Duties will be conducted within the usual set up, age mixed groups. However, since all Jungmädel of the older age groups must also master the service of the first Jungmädel age group, both, the mixed units and the year-by-year units of older age groups must work according to these guidelines.

This educational guideline here shall aid you in the fulfilment of your responsibilities. Further to this, you will receive additional inspirations from the leadership office of your Upper Gau (District).

You should always be mindful that these 10-year-olds are in their first year of service, and that everything you put towards them during this time will form them, not just for their further service but also for their whole life.

Working guidelines for the Jungmädel service for the first year

These present training guidelines define the various types of service of the Jungmädelbund, based on previous experience. In order to make the practical implementation of all the information understood, a clear example is given for each type of service. This has always been taken from the material of the first year and can be used at the appropriate time.

Overview

I. Instructions for service
   A. Implementing
   B. Examples

II. Home afternoon
   A. Implementing
      1. Basics
      2. Regulations for conducting a home afternoon
      3. Aids for the home afternoon –
         The picture material   of the H.J.
   B. Examples
      ["Our leader Adolf Hitler"]
      ["The world belongs to the happy ones]

III. Sports afternoon
  A. Implementing
    1. Basics
    2. Practical guidelines
    3. Organization of a Jungmädel sports afternoon
  B. Examples
    Sports afternoon outside
    Sports afternoon in a closed room
    Sports afternoon in a gym

IV. Practical Jungmädel work
  A. Implementing
    Singing and making music
    Playing
    Story telling
    Arts and crafts
  B. Examples

V. Trips
  A. Implementing
  B. Examples

I. Service briefings

The service briefing will be set up as a new type of service instruction. It is intended to instruct the Jungmädel about her duties and tasks, that are placed before her in the H. J. and to provide her with the necessary basic knowledge.

A. Implementation of a service briefing

Service instructions shall be conducted twice a month before the practical Jungmädel service and also before each special service and should take no longer than 20 minutes.

The service instruction must be clear and factually structured. Thus, every leader shall prepare for this carefully.

It must be ensured that the service briefing never degenerates into mere reciting and babbling. The Jungmädel must be educated to do her own thinking and speaking.

The service briefing shall be conducted in form of questions and answers. Probable topics for a service briefing shall be: What is expected of a Jungmädel? – Proper service dress.

—The organisational structure right down to the J.M. group.— In addition the most important songs and key phrases need to be learned.

There follows an example:

B. Service Briefing: Duties as a Jungmädel

At the beginning of the service briefing, the Jungmädel leader explains to her Jungmädel, that from now on, upon entry into the Hitler Youth, there will always be special requirements demanded from them.
The Jungmädelbund demands, that every Jungmädel will be brought up to a life of comradeship and duty, honesty and loyalty.

a] The Jungmädel is a good comrade:

The JM–group shall build a community. Thus, they will need to stick together and stand up for their community at all times. The commitment of each and every one is of utter importance.

Question: Where does the Jungmädel prove her comradeship?

Answer: In her Jungmädel group, where she will step up each and every time.

18

Question:	How does the Jungmädel show her comradeship?
Answer:	Always punctual for service. Helping her comrades with their homework. Helping her comrades by supporting them doing their house work, i.e. looking after smaller siblings, shopping and such like, enabling her comrade to attend the meetings regularly. Sharing of provisions during a trip. Collectively saving to buy the uniform for a less wealthy comrade. Putting aside one's own person Not pushing oneself forward and not flattering.

Examples of wrong comradeship:

Turning up late for meetings without a valid reason and thus causing interruptions.
Letting someone copy school work.
Give misinformation in order to prevent a comrade from receiving punishment.

Bad violations against comradeship:

Gaining advantages from the community, i.e., going home, while the others are still busy cleaning up the communal area or to visit a birthday party instead of a home afternoon.

Taking advantage of good-natured comrades.

Attempts of setting others into a bad light in front of the leader.

Not punctual for service.

Severe forgetfulness and inattentiveness.

b] The Jungmädel is discreet.

The Jungmädel is not a chatter box, nor does she blow her own trumpet, she is discreet.

Question: Why is the Jungmädel discreet?

Answer: These serious times do not just require a soldier to be discreet, but the same is also required from our girls and woman.

Question: How can gossiping indebt you?

Answer: A comrade can become upset, or her honor offended through careless gossip.

Answer: You do not talk about matters the Jungmädel need to sort out amongst themselves, i.e. if one of the girls has failed her group, this is to be kept away from other Jungmädel groups, it is not to be discussed outside the group.

Answer: In later life of the Jungmädel: the creation of wrong rumours and unnecessary worries, in peace time as well as during the war. The betrayal of important economic and military secrets and thus causing interruption to the work of our Führer.

c] The Jungmädel is honest and faithful.

Answer: Jungmädel shall always spring to action where needed, unconditionally so. She shall never ask about advantages or disadvantages.

Question: How does honesty present itself?

Answer: A Jungmädel behaves simple and straight forward. Competitions shall be won honestly. It is not honest to go against the rules and consciously trying to cheat.

Answer: If someone has acted stupidly and thus harmed the honor of the Jungmädel group, she will have to face the consequences more so than ever, for every single one is responsible to uphold the honor of the Jungmädelschaft. Every outsider will transport the behavior of one Jungmädel onto the whole Jungmädel group.

Question: How does a Jungmädel prove her loyalty?

Answer: By regularly attending meetings and by conscientiously fulfilling the tasks the Jungmädel service has put before her. From the very first day of attending the Jungmädelbund she has sworn allegiance to the Hitler Youth and the Führer. Thus, every girl will now fulfil her service to nation and Führer within her community.

II. Home afternoons

A. Conducting a home afternoon

1. The basics

It is our task to make our Jungmädel to be alert and open-minded, so that they are not indifferent towards the questions and events that occur in the everyday life of our nation, and that they do not look upon their Jungmädel being without the necessary earnestness. Especially in this first year, we want them to very much feel how much they belong into the community of this nation and that this nation will once be what their youth is now. We must lead them, that with this responsibility in mind, to start working on themselves. It is down to us, to take this will and the character traits that lay within each in girl and channel and form them into the right direction.

Our Führer is our idol. He stands above all of our lives and for the Jungmädel he is the ultimate portrayal of a German. And then, using the role-models of the German past, from German fairy tales and legends, we take the moral values, which have always played a great part in German life, and these shall play part in the direction of one's own life.

The same task can be seen in the German folk song. It creates a strong community and opens the mind. At the same time is a tool of expression for one's own feelings.

2. Guideline for conducting a home afternoon

All the matters we want to teach our Jungmädel will be discussed during a home afternoon. Here we will answer all their questions that may have arisen from their lively interest towards all matters concerning life. The home evening should always be lively and also stay that way. It should never be pressed into a rigid form. Thus, there cannot be a finite and binding way. The progress of the Jungmädel group will always be the decisive factor. Considerations for the preparation of a home afternoon: Preparations must never be superficial, just as the preparation of the subject itself must never be superficial. The guidelines for conducting a home afternoon can be found in the home evenings magazine of the Reichs Youth leadership "Die Jungmädelschaft", which contains songs, poems and stories.

When dealing with a topic we always start with the closest thing that our Jungmädel really understands.

Song and speech, which underline the theme of the home afternoon, will always start us off. To be followed by a story or one's own narrative. We will encourage our Jungmädel to help shape the afternoon. They will present stories, tell tales and show pictures to enhance the subject matter. Every girl may report about something they have experienced themselves, heard from their parents or siblings or have read somewhere. In doing so, we wake their own interest and achieve that they will not just pay attention to the matter during the two hours of the home afternoon but will be on the lookout for the matter and thus build a connection between their home afternoon and their own life. Thus, we create a unit between our teachings and the daily life and experiences of our Jungmädel.

A final song completes each home afternoon.

The framework for the home afternoon, set out in the following guidelines, is binding for all units of the Jungmädel groups.

1. The JM leader prepares the home afternoon meticulously.

2. The JM leader responsible for the room will, each month, nominate a few Jungmädel who will, clean, air and heat the room.

3. The home afternoon will always start on time.

4. The home evening is classed as service and must be attended in uniform.

5. If someone is late, they greet quietly, without causing a disturbance and will make their apologies at the end of the home afternoon.

6. Keeping of the service book, collecting membership fees and any necessary orders are to be done at the beginning of the home afternoon and must take no longer than 15 minutes.

7. The home afternoon definitely starts with a song and also ends with a song.

8. The circle that attends the home afternoon should only consist of one JM group.

9. The room, if weather permits, should always be entered as a group and left as a group once the home afternoon has concluded.

10. We refrain from using tables, they will only pose as disruptive. Instead, we will set the chairs up in a circle.

11. The leader of the home afternoon shall try and get as many Jungmädel involved in the layout as possible, as long as this does not hamper the success. The leader of the home afternoon will lead through the afternoon in a strict and firm manner. Reasons for the poor execution of the home afternoon are often lack of concentration.

12. We will always strive to educate using our own words. We will only read to our group when we are quoting our Führer or Reichs Youth leader, or if the text in front of us has been poetically designed, or if our own reciting does not give the text gratitude. We consciously cultivate our innate gift of narration.

3. Aids for the home afternoon – The HJ picture aids.

The "Picture books for educating the Hitler youth" (filmstrips) are designed to aid the vivid and lively presentation of the home afternoon and should be shown using the HJ picture device.

a] How do we get hold of these aids?

The picture books, each consisting of 36 pictures, including their accompanying brochure, costs 1 RM per piece, excluding delivery and can be obtained directly from the Reichsjugendführung, Verwaltungsamt, Einkauf, Bildbanddienst, W35, Kurfürstenstr. 35. The picture aid service will issue two new picture books per month. Each group or several groups together can subscribe to these picture aids for 2.50 RM per month. Subscriptions directly to the address above.

The HJ picture device – a projector with 250-Watt output – consistent of the basic device, with lamp, stage resistant measure, spare light bulb and transport case, costs 100,- RM and can be obtained from specialist dealers. If this device is not available, it can be hired from Jungbann, or one can try to borrow one from another organization or school to use during the home afternoon.

b] How to present
An instruction manual is glued to the inside of the lid; this is to be read carefully before use. This contains clear instructions of how to connect the device and how to insert to picture books. A white

wall surface will suffice for projection, this should however have smooth plaster, or one can make a projection surface using stiff paper or a white sheet of 1.50 metre x 1 metre in size.

Before usage the voltage needs to be established, for if this is wrong, the bulb will burn out and 12,- RM would have been wasted. The matt side of the picture books, the so-called shift side, must be kept safe from dust, dirt, wet fingers and hard objects. Before returning the device to its case, both parts must have completely cooled down. The connecting cable can then be wrapped around the device and the resistor.

For the Jungmädel of the first year the following picture books are of importance:

> Adolf Hitler
> Germany awakens
> German Christmas
> How our ancestors lived
> German history, an obligation

The HJ picture projector belongs into each home of the Hitler Youth. Every Jungmädel leader can work this device. The picture books bring beautiful and poignant pictures and maps, that have been fused together with words and themes and will easily be understood by every Jungmädel. In addition, the accompanying leaflet will provide the Jungmädel leader with information in order to provide further explanations and to be able to answer questions.

B. Example of a home afternoon

1. Home afternoon:

Subject: Our Führer Adolf Hitler

Speaker: There is one right in this world and this right is: one's own strength.
[Adolf Hitler]

Song: Auf, hebt unsere Fahnen

Reading: The greatest about him is: Not only is he our leader, and for many a hero, his is himself: Straight, firm and humble. In him rest the worries of our world and his soul brushed against the stars, and yet he remained human, just like you and me.
[Baldur von Schirach]

Narrative: If we look at our Führer's first years of life, we can see that even the young Adolf Hitler can be a role model, for during this time his indomitable will, strength, bravery, comradeship and a zest for life and a huge interest on matter concerning the nation, already distinguished him.

Reading: The home town of Adolf Hitlers ancestors is situated within a beautiful landscape of fertile soil, stunning forests and small winding creeks. It is the "Lower Austrian Forest

29

district", situated between the Danube and the southern tip of the Sudetenland, which has already been returned home.

Alois Hitler grew up in one of the villages of the forest district, in Spital, during the last century, as the son of his father Adolf Hitler, a smallholder. The young Alois Hitler felt compelled to leave his small world and to better himself out there in the big, wide world and to get himself a good position. His tireless zest for work helped him overcome all obstacles, and at the age of twenty-three he became a civil servant with the customs authorities. He was posted to Braunau by the Inn. And here, in this little town, in the Ostmark, once part of Bavaria and thus of the German Reich, our Führer Adolf Hitler was born on 20.Apri 1889.

The house Adolf Hitler was born in was by no means a palace, but an ordinary small south German house. The cradle in which he laid was not surrounded by wealth and opulence. The parents who looked after and watched over the young life, were humble, honest and healthy people, who had given their boy the best of their own good dispositions in life.

Narrative: When Adolf Hitler's father retired, he bought himself a farm in Hafeld, next the market town of Lambach by the Traun, in upper Austria, farming the estate himself. This is where Adolf Hitler, son of a civil servant, became a farmer's son. He learned, just like his father, and together with his young comrades, to value the farmer himself, the hard, arduous work, the love of the land and the fields. But he also learned about hardship and poverty, not all of it was pleasure. This young boy, with his lively character and inquisitive mind did not spend his time at home. His playgrounds were the thick forests, the wide fields, the nature around him. But over and over again he found comrades that caused especially his mother some concern. For these comrades, lots of robust boys, who despite being only children, were quite weathered and always up for an adventure. Adolf Hitler had quickly become the ringleader who was leading the groups forays in the surrounding areas. Not only had he grown to be a strapping young farmers boy, but he was also far more intelligent than any of them and even at this young age, his extraordinary talent as a speaker was clearly recognizable. He used it to mediate between his always arguing comrades. And not even his father, sending him to secondary school in Lambach because of the better schooling, could not stop him. School was easy to him, but travel to and from school took up two hours a day. Not a problem in summer, but in winter, with the snow laying knee-deep and in addition that ice cold wind blowing sharpish from the mountains, made the walk to school quite arduous and dangerous for a boy.

In spring 1898 life changed again for the Hitler family when Hitler's father sold the farm in Hafeld and bought a flat in Lambach in "Schmid's Mühle". Adolf Hitler, nine years old at the time, found a new circle of comrades and once more, fought "wild battles" with his mates.

Once again, he led all the adventures, be it in the old mill or outside in the open. During these games and arguments, the basis of the being the leader was already evident, for even as a young boy, he was ready to achieve his will using physical strength. His readiness to fight would later, as a political leader, enable him to follow his path, once he had decided it was the right one, without consideration.

This readiness to fight and preparedness has no doubt caused his mother some sorrow and probably also additional work, mending torn trousers, socks and jackets and also tending lovingly to the bruises and wounds the boy had received. But during all this time he never neglected his educational obligations. He was always up there with the best. Learning was easy to him, and thus left him plenty of time for the desired adventures.

On 3. January 1903, when Adolf Hitler was thirteen, his father, seemingly healthy and strong, died suddenly of a stroke.

Then, at the age of sixteen, he also lost his mother.

After the death of his parents and by then totally impoverished, Hitler made his way to Vienna to train as a master builder. He knew that life would be tough, but he was determined to succeed. The carefree time of his childhood had come to an end. He came to Vienna without money, friends or relatives that could have helped. He needed money and that straight away, as not to go hungry, and the only way was to work. Adolf Hitler worked on a building site and thus learned about the working man's life. He also learned that the working men would be chased off the sites by the Jews. During these times, poverty was a constant companion. Life did improve when he went to Munich. Here he drew and painted and earned money through his artwork. While in Vienna and in Munich, Hitler read a lot.

Reading: When the great war started, Hitler felt, that he too, just like thousands of others, should volunteer to go to war for Germany. As an Austrian national he would have had to serve with the Austrian brothers in arms, but he did not see the Habsburger government as a suitable defender of all matters German, and thus, after permission by the Bavarian King himself, joined the Bavarian Reserve Infantry Regiment 16 for service at the front. This regiment was named the "List" regiment, after its first commander. Hitler was assigned as the regimental message runner, an often difficult and also very responsible task, for messages had to be received fast, for the fate and the positions of his comrades often depended on the prompt and correct delivery of the message. Only reliable and brave men, that would not hesitate, would be used for these duties. Quite often Hitler's path was accompanied by the sounds of drum fire and his path across the battlefield would become a race with death. At the end of 1914 he had already been awarded the Iron Cross Class II.

The reason why Private Hitler had not been promoted to group leader can be explained that the staff of his regiment did not want to lose this brave and reliable battle orderly. Adolf Hitler never went on leave. Never, and he also took on the duties of his other comrades, so they were able to return home to their families. He didn't have anybody to send him a parcel or a letter, anyone who thought of him, not even at Christmas. His comrades held him in high esteem because of his bravery and his helpful nature.

During the last few weeks of the great war, the fearless messenger Adolf Hitler, thought off as invulnerable by his comrades, committing his life for our nation, had his efforts at the front brought to an end by a British gas attack. Shortly before the attack he was awarded the Iron Cross Class I for his bravery.

For he had received orders to reconnoitre the remains of a village near the river arm of the Wytschäte, to see if the enemy had settled there. Accompanied by only one comrade, he went back and forth to the front a hundred times – into grenade and machine gun fire. Doing what his commander deemed necessary until the situation was clear: Are they Germans or Frogs laying in that wrecked, by grenades destroyed village? Both messengers listened, lurked, crawled on their bellies – a broken wall here – a well locked door in a ruined house there – let's go. Break it open! Oh – bugger. Frogs! Six, seven, eight and more. Fifteen men! That's it?!

Adolf Hitler, however, shouted at the frogs, while firing a shot through the air: "Give up!" He waved behind his back, as if hundreds of men were to follow to arrest the surprised mob. It was that wave which persuaded the French to surrender their arms and when they entered daylight, they were surprised to find out that one German singlehandedly had taken out a whole troop. A haggard, pale, tired out private, who was now driving his prisoners in front of him until he reached his regimental staff.

2. Home afternoon

"The world belongs to the happy ones" (amusing stories and jesters' tales)

Examples for a funny, amusing home afternoon, just as it should be conducted for the Jungmädel group.

For this we select the 1. home afternoon of the month of February in the Jungmädel year.

Song:

Jung bin ich, jung bleib ich	*I am young, will stay young*
was scheren mich die Sorgen	*don't care about the worries*
und hab ich kein Glück nicht	*and if I don't have any luck*
so tu ich mir' s borgen	*I will borrow some*
Geh auf und geh nieder	*Go up and go down*
und kehre stets wieder zurück	*and always bounce back*
bin also frei	*thus, I am free*
wie ein Vogel in Ei	*just like a bird in its egg*

A Jungmädel recites:

Onwards and upwards,
don't be irked,
just tackle all sorrows that lurk around the corner.

The JM leader speaks:

Today we shall have a fun day. I will tell you many a funny tale, and I will not lie, when I report about some funny and most peculiar things that have happened. Rogues and scallywags have once reported these tales and antics to me, the pranks of "Till Eulenspiegel" and "Münchhausen". There are that many that I am not sure where to start.

I will begin with the peculiar adventures of the Baron of Münchhausen.

So here it goes:

The JM tells the story:

How the horse got onto the church steeple and fire comes from Münchhausen's eyes.

I started my trip in the middle of winter, travelling by horse, which, once horse and rider have taken to one another, is quite a comfortable way to travel. I rode until night and darkness settled in.

There was no village in sight and no sound to be heard. The whole land was covered in thick snow, and I could see neither street nor path. Tired of riding I dismounted my horse and tied it to a stake that stuck out of the snow. I took my pistol with me, just for safety and laid my tired head to rest in the snow not far from my horse and took such a deep sleep that my eyes did not open again until it was daylight. Much to my surprise, as I looked around me, I had woken in a beautiful village, right in the middle of the church yard. But where was my horse? It was nowhere to be seen, but suddenly I heard a whinny. It came from up above. As I looked up, I saw my horse tied to the weather wane of the church tower, hanging down by its reins. I suddenly fathomed that the village must have been covered in snow on my arrival and what I mistook for a fencepost must have been the tip of the church tower. Whilst asleep the weather must have turned and the snow must have melted, making me sink to the floor and leaving the poor horse hanging. Never one to hang about I aimed for the holster, took one shot and my trusted steed accompanied me once more.

One day I looked out of the window from my sleeping quarters only to see that the pond not far away was covered with wild ducks. I grabbed my rifle out from the corner, quickly jumped down the stairs, and went head over heels and knocked my head on the doorframe. Fire and sparks shot from my eyes, but even that couldn't stop me. I was about to fire a shot, when I come to realize that the stone had come off my firing cock. Oh, what to do? No time to waste. Just as well I remembered what had happened to my eyes just now. So, I opened the pan, put the rifle straight to one eye, launched my fist at the other. This created enough sparks to set off the gun powder and with an almighty bang, the gun fired and shortly after I could call 5 pairs of ducks, four rednecks and a couple of coots my own. Presence of the spirit is precisely the soul of manly deeds.

And next I will tell you a funny story about the adventures of the seven men from Swabia:

The leader reads:

The adventures of the seven men from Swabia:

There once were seven men from Swabia who got together to go on a trip. But before they set off, each and every one of them went to purchase one special item to take with them. The one with the fancy buttons bought a roasting spit, the one from the Allgäu bought a storm hat with a feather and the one with the yellow feet bought a set of spurs for his boots. Seehas bought himself a harness with the comment "One can never be too careful." The Swabian with the mirror agreed and said he would wear one too. After they had been walking for quite some time, with many adventures already behind them, they got to a forest by Überlingen, near Lake Constance, said to be haunted by a monster which they wanted to tackle.

How the seven men from Swabia get into battle formation.

It was time for the seven Swabians to set up battle formation. Seehas was of the opinion that they should all line up next to each other, like they always did. The Swabian with the fancy buttons agreed and said there should be no changes.

But the Allgäuer insisted on a change, saying that just for once he wanted to come last and not first.

"Bravery", said the quick Swabian, "I have a lot of this in my flesh, belief you me, but there isn't enough flesh for me to be brave enough to put up with a monster." The little Swabian asked: "Why does there have to be a first and a last, can we just not all stay in the middle? That way none of us will get hurt."

"And I am of the opinion," said the Swabian with the mirror, " it will be best if one sacrifices himself for all. – Button Swabian, what do you think? You look just right for the task. You would provide a good meal."

But that one started to scream and stamp and gesticulate on all fours, just as if he had already been put on the spit.

This caused Seehas to address his fellow wayfarers: " Dear friends and compatriots! Freshly drawn is half fought. Nothing is better than bravery defeating evil. A good heart will defeat all evil. Desperate, honorable men never came of the plane."

Said, and turned to the one with the yellow feet:

"Well cock, you will lead the way.

You have boots and spurs

so the rabbit will not be able to bite you!"

And the one with the yellow feet let himself to be convinced and though: Either I will hunt the animal and it will run, or the animal will hunt me, and I will run. That way we will never, ever catch up with each other our whole life long.

So let it be known that the seven men from Swabia headed towards the undergrowth, slowly, slowly, carefully heading towards each bush, and when they arrived at the one, of which Seehas said houses the dragons' nest, the Swabian with the mirror suddenly said: "I have pains in my stomach, I am stepping aside."

The Allgäuer didn't like this at all and told him to stay where he was and join in with the efforts.

The Swabian with the mirror answered that he was stepping aside to spy, to see where the animal may be.

"Don't bother," answered the Allgäuer, "I will tell you where it is, you stay. Be told!"

"You all stay where you are and shut up," shouted Seehas. "Just keep eyes and ears open!

And as they come closer to the bush, oh look, a little hare. The hare sits up, snuffles, jumps up and runs away. The seven Swabians almost freeze in front of the bush – in astonishment.

"Did you see that; did you see it?" They cried out loud, one after the other. "It's huge. Like a poodle, like an ox, like a camel," one shouted after the other.

"What are you saying?" shouted the Allgäuer. If that wasn't a hare, I cannot distinguish one mountain from another anymore!"

"Well, what?" answered Seehas. "It's neither here nor there, this hare is larger than all of them together."

> So there stands at the end of each place,
> the indisputably true sentence:
> The difficulty is always small
> man, just doesn't have to be prevailed!

[Wilhelm Busch]

Song: „Ich will Euch erzählen und auch nicht lügen, ich sah ein paar gebratene Tauben fliegen."

„Let me tell you, and I won't lie, I have just seen a pair of roasted pigeons flying by."

42

or: Husaren kommen reiten,   *Hussars are approaching*
        den Säbel an der Seiten!   *The sabre to their side!*
        Hau dem Schelm ein Ohr ab,   *take off the rogues ear,*
        Hau's ihm nicht zu dicht ab!   *but don't take it off to close!*
        Lass ihm noch ein Stücklein   *Leave a little bit left over,*
        dran, damit man den   *so that the rogue can be*
        Schelm erkennen kann.   *identified.*

The JM leader speaks:

And finally, I will tell you the tale of Eulenspiegel and his funny rope dance. Have you all heard of Eulenspiegel and his mother? No? – You will now get to listen to his adventures.

So, sit still and listen carefully.

The JM leader begins:

How Eulenspiegel dances on a rope and is being ridiculed.

Eulenspiegel's mother lived in a house where the courtyard back on to the Saale. And Eulenspiegel started walking on a tight robe. He did this in the attic of the house at first, for he did not want his mother to see – for she would not tolerate this stupidity of him walking the rope and she had already threatened to smack him. And once she did catch him and took to hand a big stick trying to bash him off the rope, but he escaped through the window and sat on the roof where she couldn't get to him.

This carried on until he got a little older and once again, he started playing on the tight rope. This time he pulled it from his mother's house across the Saale to a house on the other side. And plenty of people, young and old, became aware of the rope and that Eulenspiegel was planning to walk across it. They came and wanted to watch and wondered what he might be up to. And just as Eulenspiegel sat on the rope, with his performance at its best, his mother came home. She went up into the attic, from where the rope was fastened tight and cut through it. Eulenspiegel, her son fell into the water and took a bath in the Saale, much ridiculed by all his spectators. The farmers laughed and the young boys shouted:

"Hey, keep swimming, you are long overdue a bath!" This upset Eulenspiegel and albeit he did not care much about being in the water, but he took much notice of the insolence the young boys hurdled at him and wondered how he could take revenge and thus he kept on swimming and pondering.

Eulenspiegel takes revenge.

Shortly thereafter Eulenspiegel decided to take revenge and pulled the tight rope from a different house across the Saale and announced to the good folk of his town that he intended to walk the rope once more. As the crowds grew, he spoke to the young boys and asked each of them for their left shoe; he wanted to show them a trick, those were his words and young and old lifted their foot, took off their shoe and handed it to him. Eulenspiegel collected two shoes, that is two times sixty. All shoes were tied together in a long row, and he climbed onto the rope with them.

Once he got to the middle of the rope, everybody assumed they would see a fine trick.

Some the young ones however got impatient and wished they had their shoe back. Eulenspiegel sat down in the middle of the rope and shouted: "Take note, take note, and look for your shoe!" And with that he cut the strings apart and let all the shoes fall to the floor. They all ended up in a big heap and young and old darted towards them, looking for their shoes. One picked one up here and another there. One said: "This shoe is mine!" Another answered: "No, you are lying, it's mine!" And they started arguing and fell at one another and began to fight. One was on the floor, the other on top of him; one shouted, the other cried, a third laughed and this carried on until the old ones handed out smacks across the heads and pulled at their hair. And Eulenspiegel watched from his rope and laughed: "Now look for your shoes, just like you made me swim yesterday." He jumped off the rope and ran off, leaving the old and the young to argue over their shoes. As he could not be seen in front of the young and the old for the next four weeks he sat at home at his mother's and much to her delight he mended Helmstädter shoes. She hoped that her boy had cut a corner, little did she know what he had been up to and the real reason why he did not want to leave the house.

Final Song: So geht es in dem Schnützelputz-Häusel
da singen und tanzen die Mäusel....
da bellen die Schnecken im Häusel
Im Schnützelputz-Häusel da geht es sehr toll da
saufen die Tische und Bänke sich voll
Pantoffeln unter dem Bette

This is how it works in the Schnützelputz-Häusel
where the mice sing and dance....
the snails bark,
Things are going very well in the Schnützelputz-
Häusel the tables and benches are getting drunk
Slippers under the bunk

III. Sports afternoon

A. Conducting a sports afternoon
1. The basics

When we see a big, long way ahead of us during our work at the end of which the healthy, true girl stands, then sport is an essential part of this big journey, because it determines the whole person in her outer shape and makes her ready and receptive.

When the girls come to us at the age of 10, it is the job of the JM leader to put the common experience at the center of the education. This applies to sports as well as to any other work. Especially in sports we have the means to do this better than anywhere else. Every girl has a natural sense of movement but has to develop this in every way. Our task is to steer it in the right direction and thus make sport a real physical e d u c a t i o n.

The JM leader puts her stamp on the unit that she leads. It is up to her to inspire and provide the means for physical education. If she tackles her task fresh and firm, the young girls will also be happy with the task in hand. Because of that, every sports lesson must be carefully prepared.

Every guide needs to know the following basic things before a JM sports session:

Jungmädel are in the process of p h y s i c a l d e v e l o p m e n t and therefore tire very easily. Hence excessive athletic stress is unsuitable, because their strength is not yet sufficient to carry out duration and strength exercises for a longer period of time. Strenuous and continuous work should particularly be avoided during this growing season. Exercises with short, rapid force followed by a break from time to time during which the body can recover, are appropriate and promote the development of the whole organism.

It is also important that the young girls always show a good posture, so that they do not develop round or hollow backs. For this reason, support exercises on devices or a backwards bridge are to be avoided at all costs. In JM sport, games will form the basis of physical education.

Think about the games and fighting games, that should not be missing in any sports lesson. Such a game only has real value if it is carried out correctly. Every Jungmädel has to fulfil her task within the game and has to absolutely obey the rules of the game. The leader has to pay close attention to this. If the Jungmädel do all they can to lead their team to victory, the game must be strictly disciplined, despite the zeal and liveliness.

After using games as the basis of JM sport, the elementary school of physical exercises, including JM gymnastics, track and field sports, swimming, floor gymnastics, obstacle gymnastics and Jungmädel dance will be introduced. Competitive sports do not yet exist for ten-year-old girls. A specific task is set for each quarter.

1. quarter: JM gymnastics and athletics stand in the foreground, for the ten-year-old girl has to compete in the Reich Sport event and also take her JM test. - In athletics (throwing, jumping running and so on) the performance should be increased very gradually. - In summer, the 10-year-old girls participate at the sports festivals of the Hitler Youth possibly also in JM dancing.

2. quarter: The young girls shall learn the basics of swimming, or at least make friends with the water.

3. quarter: The focus is on floor exercises.

4. quarter: The focus is on obstacle exercises. For this, all existing equipment such as balance beams, bars, ladders, boxes, balls, etc. can be used. Conducting obstacle running, the young girls get to know these devices, how to overcome them, have to muster courage, skill and speed.

Order training generally forms part of the JM Sport.

2. Practical instructions

In the country side the Jungmädel sports service is conducted in Jungmädelschaften or Jungmädelscharen, in towns in Jungmädel groups. The Jungmädel sports service is lead and conducted by the Jungmädel leader herself.

In summer, the sport service is held on sports fields, in the country on playgrounds or fields.

Swimming may only be carried out in bathing establishments under the supervision of lifeguards, or in waters approved for swimming. In winter, the practice site is the gym. In the countryside, if there is no gym, a larger pub hall shall be used. If there is a covered swimming pool, swimming should also be included into the sports service during winter.

3. Structure of a Jungmädel sports afternoon.

The Jungmädel sports afternoon divides as follows:

a) Preparatory Exercises
b) Main Training
c) Games

Example (Summer and winter):

a) Preparatory Exercises (10 – 15 minutes)

As preparatory exercises we use Jungmädel gymnastics, which is carried out together with all young girls at the beginning of each class. The exercises are put together in such a way that the whole body is worked through according to plan.

b) Main Training (25 minutes)

The main training is carried out in several groups (teams), which are put together according to the capabilities of the young girls. It is important to achieve a specific training goal during main training.

In Summer	In Winter
Track and field athletics	Floor exercises
Swimming	Obstacle gymnastics

c) Games (15 – 20 minutes)

At the end of each session, games or relays are conducted to get all the Jungmädel together again.

B. Example for a sports afternoon

1. Sports afternoon outside

In spring and summer, the sport service is held outside, if possible, in the country a free space is sought in a meadow or outside in the forest. All the girls are always busy, no one is allowed to stand around or feel uninvolved in any way. It has to be so lively that nobody even thinks about getting bored.

Everyone lines up and starts counting.
A song is sung to start with.

Running:
Everyone runs towards circle. Does ordinary running, running with knees raised, running with the lower legs hitting the upper. Add in as much variety as possible.

Running backwards. Make sure that you take big strides. Then run forward again. Change commands often:

Forwards, backwards, turn and keep running. Etc.

Now comes a pause to catch breath: raise arms slowly, lift from the side, breathe out, let your arms and upper body fall forward and exhale audibly. (long breath out).

Then start running again.

In the forest, scatter freely around the trees, over fences and ditches, a tall girl running last, who makes sure that everyone keeps up. Walk in between.

Find a suitable place to conduct a f a r j u m p, if possible, with a ditch or a path to jump over it. If there are too many girls, divide into groups of ten, by all means let them jump free at first, then run up, take-off and over. Some always jump with both feet when they want to jump across an obstacle. They run up and just before the jump they stop and almost stand still and then do the  final jump over the ditch. With these you will need to practice especially on level ground, the other jump in time over a wider part of the ditch.

Do this for 15 - 20 minutes, then back to the starting point. It is time to play games now.

Numbers race

All girls are being divided into teams. If there are 60 Jungmädel it will make 10 teams.

Every team gets a number and every girl in the team gets a number too, in every team. The numbers go from 1 to 6. One girl is the captain, the teams stand in a star circle around the captain, in the middle lies an object, for example a shoe or a cap.

Now the captain calls up a number, for example number 5. Then all girls with the number 5 run once around the circle and then into the middle and try to get the object in the middle as quickly as possible. Whoever gets it first, receives one point for her team, and at the end of the game all points are added together. The team that has the most points, wins.

Standing ball

All the girls are lined up in a circle. In the middle there is a girl standing in a small, marked out square.

If you need 2 to 3 balls to play, the girls try to drive the one in the middle out of the square using the balls. The balls are rolled on the floor, the girl in the middle must not be touched by the balls. Is the girl driven out of the square or has been touched by one of the balls, all the girls run away until the girl in the middle has caught the ball and calls out "stop". Now she must try to hit one of the girls. Whoever is hit by the ball must now enter the square.

2. Sports afternoon in closed rooms

The prerequisite is that there is no gym. A hall or a large guest room is being used.

Line up in one line – count through.
A song is sung to begin with.

It starts with light gymnastics. It should be simple but work through the whole body.

Line-up:
In rows of four. The leader who indicates the exercises and demonstrates it, must stand in such a way that she can be seen by all the girls.

Command:
All commands must be given clearly and firmly.

Exercises taken from the Jungmädel gymnastics:

Jumping jack: Jump into a side straddle and back again. While jumping, the hands are clasped over the head, when jumping back they are brought back into the side position, when jumping up slightly flex the knees.

Basic position: Let yourself fall into the crouch position, then jump out of the crouch by pulling up your arms, move into a straight jump and then immediately crouch again.

Sit down: Without the help of your arms, get up and immediately return into a seated position. To make things more difficult, have your arms crossed in front of your body.

Seat: Stretch, arms by your sides, slowly raise your legs at the same time and then slowly lower them again. Particular attention should be paid to breathing here.

Stretch seat: Bend quickly with your legs clasping your arms, crouching your legs together, then straighten your legs again, straighten your body, holding your arms to the side.

Lie down: With arms close to your body. The body is completely stretched, turning with momentum so that one is in the prone position and turning again on ones back, once on the left, once on the right.

Back position: Bend your legs slightly, tip of toe above your head, swing back again, then both legs above your head with your knees coming up close to your ears, up into the stand.

Starting position: Arms to the side. Storch walk, slowly lifting a bent leg up, stretching the lower leg, upper body slightly forward, put the stretched leg down, followed by the standing leg . Do the same with the other leg starting with the left leg.

Starting position: Fall into the crouch position, hands are propped up in front of the body and run with your hands forward until the body is stretched into the push-up position. The feet remain firmly on the ground. Do the same with your legs. Knees straight.

Break – Song

Gymnastics exercises or games. Floor gymnastic mats can be made by yourself. Button tent panels together and fill with straw. Simple rolls of somersaults forwards and backwards. Handstands with two girls. One girl goes to the bench. Handstand over the bench. Give assistance. When doing a handstand over the bench, she guides the practitioner's head with the right hand and helps swing the body over with the left. The hands are placed in front of the bench.

Roll over obstacles: The hands are placed behind the kneeling girl, head is drawn in, chin on the chest, make a round and roll up, into the stand.

More accomplished girls will try this over 2 or 3 girls sitting close together.

Dancing in twos or threes.
Walking like a crab.

All mimic the centipede crawl and then assemble.

Break – song

Games – Page 108
       1) Running Games – page 108
       2) Bustling Games – page 111
       3) Ball Games in Circle – page 112
       4) Ball Games and Relay – page 115

3. Sports afternoon in the gym

Line-up, straighten out, count through.
Song.

Divide into four groups. Running games.

1. Each group gets a mat and puts it in a corner of the gym. The whole team stands on the mat. At the  whistle team 1 and 3 and 2 and 4 respective, change places. (And of course we do not bump into each other).

The team that is back on the mat first, is the winner. The game can be changed. All girls kneel on the mat, or everyone is sitting on it. Then you can change places 1 with 4 and 2 with 3, and also the method of running. Use many changes such as frog or dog run, etc. This running game can of course also be played without a mat, where an appropriate place is marked on the ground for each team.

2. Form a circle in the middle of the hall, touch hands and walk around until the whistle sounds, then everyone diverges and hangs from or stands on a device, feet away from the floor. Who

was last to touch the floor? That girl is eliminated and helps the game leader to look out.

3. Now we will do partner exercises:

Draw a thick line of chalk through the middle of the gym and then set up in double formation to the right and left of the line.

First there is a **pull fight**. The right foot is allowed to be close to the drawn line; the hands are grasped and now everyone tries to pull their partner over the line. Who is the strongest?

Then a **push fight**: Put your hands against each other and try to push your partner back to get across the line yourself, determine the winner and let them compete against each other again. The eliminated ones sit around cheering the others on and the game continues on until the strongest of the group is determined.

4. Sit back-to-back in a line, hook your arms together and stand up, you can count; 1 stand up 2 sit down. When everyone can do this, count the individual pairs by two. On 1 couple 1 gets up and sits down on 2, then couple 2 gets up and sits down on 1. This goes in turns.

5. Sit in pairs, tips of the toes together, hands together, arms stretched and stand up together. Now do this alternating. One girl sits, the other stands. Alternate between sitting down and standing up. It should look like a seesaw! One girl sits down; the other gets up.

6. To finish off, a skill exercise. The task is to stand opposite each other as a pair. Hold hands and try climbing through, which pair is skilled and can do it without letting go of their hands?

To finish the session, we will sing and dance two dances:

Widewitt, my man has come – Page 218
The Spielman – Page 221

IV. Practical Jungmädel Work

A. Implementation

Practical Jungmädel work is to be conducted twice a month.

It consists of:

1. Singing and making music
2. Games
3. Story telling
4. Crafting

The afternoon set aside for practical Jungmädel work is to be filled with either singing or making music, telling stories, playing games or handicrafts.

It is important to cultivate and promote the natural talent of the Jungmädel for all these things and to give the Jungmädel a clear direction. Very planned work is required for this.

B. Example

There is no need to cite a particular example for singing and making music, songs to be performed, singing games, charades and home games. Explanations can be found in the material collection for the first year on page 97.

Below is an example of craft work.

We fold a drinking beaker!

The leader
Prepares the crafts afternoon thoroughly. First of all, it is important to ensure that there are enough tables and chairs in a room, because it is necessary that every Jungmädel has her own workplace. A paper drinking cup shall be folded from a sheet of 20 x 20 centimetres (8") in size. A pile of sheets of the same size, befitting the amount of Jungmädel must be ready.

The Jungmädel
Enter the home afternoon room and sing a traveling song. Next the leader tells them what they will need for a day trip. So as not to take too many things with you in your haversack, she suggests folding a paper drinking cup. All the young girls will make this themselves, the leader takes a sheet of paper, the Jungmädels too, and now the process is followed according to the leader's instructions:

"We place the square in front of us so that one corner points to the edge of the table. Now we fold the sheet together so that it forms a triangle. The break line ends with the edge of the table. Now the top tip folds onto the break line. We press down on the break line firmly with our thumb. Now the sheet is turned over and the second corner is also folded down. There are still 2 corners remaining, left and right. We insert one under the triangular flap and smooth the side edge tightly down, then turn it. Turn the whole paper over, then place the side tip under the protruding flap to create another indent at the top. If we now take the cup in one hand and squeeze the sides together a little, a lot of water or milk can fit in there."

During this first craft exercise, it is important that the Jungmädel are able to follow precise specifications. It is wrong to let any mistakes slip away. Of course it would be different in a free handicraft session. This is why we always want to think about the goal to be achieved during every afternoon and then set the task in such a way that it is achievable. In this case, every ten-year-old girl can fold such a drinking beaker.

A drinking cup like this will soon be ready and the Jungmädel will enjoy trying out more small folding work. The leader has therefore already provided the necessary material. Now let's start trying out something new.

A little box:

A square is cut out of cardboard. This is folded in half and each half sheet once more through the middle. Repeat the same with the other side of the sheet,

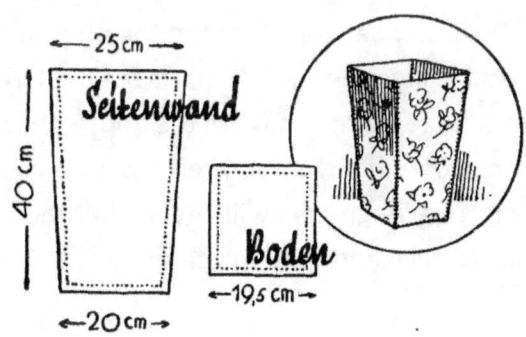

63

creating 16 small squares. Now a pair of scissors is taken, and the square cut in on each side up to the next edge. Then the outermost strip is folded up to the first line and at the break, the protruding strip is placed at right angles on the following one, so that when all 4 corners are done, we have a box instead of the sheet. Should this have a lid? You can create such a thing, which, however, has to be a bit larger overall, so that it can be put over the other box. Such small boxes, perhaps made with coloured paper or painted in bright colours, are ideal for raffles and as a gift when out in the field, especially if they contain a little surprise.

A house:
Postcards are useful for many things, i.e. – for folding a small house. Postcards can be used again quite well to depict a village or a farm. A postcard is folded lengthwise, then both halves to the middle. Now we turn the sheet over and fold the narrow sides on top of each other and again both halves to the middle, so that there are 16 small rectangles, cut up to the first line, and then push the two inner squares on top of each other to create a small roof. The outer parts are brought together that far, that they form a vertical wall to the roof. All parts are held together with a paper clip or sample clamp. To finish the house, the same is done on the other narrow side. Now you can draw windows on and put a red roof on. The Jungmädel will know what the houses in their local region look like and they will be decorated accordingly.

There are even more possibilities if you let your imagination run. One or the other Jungmädel will no doubt know a new way and so you will always do new things with scissors and paper.

Fold and cut:
If you fold a piece of paper and cut out an outline, you will discover a symmetrical shape when you unfold it. In this way you can easily make figures and trees, they can also stand freely if you move the break edge upwards and not cut through. However, it is necessary that you use durable cardboard paper for this purpose, because thin paper is inherent and would collapse.

You can easily produce very fine, delicate scissor cuts out of tissue paper, which can be used for various purposes. Napkins with delicate patterns, greeting cards and programs for fairy tale evenings with all kinds of shapes and flowers are even more beautiful when they are decorated in this way.
Our festivities during the course of the year give us a lot of inspiration for all sorts of signs and imaginary images, that can provide us with suggestions to make our paper cuttings really lively.

These can also be used as wall and book decorations. However, we should then take some black silhouette paper, which stands out particularly well against a light background, unites flowers, people and animals with the old symbols of folk art and thus offer us many opportunities to invent new things and create beautiful pictures.

V. Field Trips

A. Implementation

1. Every young girl is obliged to take part in a one-day trip once a month. This must be finished at the latest by 19:00 hours in summer, and at 18:00 hours in winter. Trips may only be

carried out within the area of the responsible JM Untergau, because every young girl should get to know the region close to her. The city Untergaue will venture into the neighbouring JM Untergaue in the countryside.

2. Walking achievements - Overall achievement 8 km (5 miles). Speed 3 km (1 mph) per hour.

Luggage: one lunch pack

After every hour of walking, you should take at least a quarter of an hour break, which is intended for relaxation only. The smallest Jungmädel should always lead the way, always set the pace of the march. Participation in bike rides is strictly forbidden.

3. Even a one-day trip has to be prepared down to the last detail. The following is to be noted:

The parents are to be informed by the Jungmädel about the duration and destination of the journey.

4. Every Jungmädel knows what travel equipment to bring with her: bread bag, field bottle, drinking cup, food, sports equipment.

5. The Jungmädel leader carries the health service bag with her.

6. The Jungmädel leader has taken a close look at the route of her hike on the map.

7. The leader takes on certain things from various fields of education for the young girls, which are to be worked out on the journey.

There are plenty of possibilities:

Singing
Singing games
Story telling
Home tales and stories that are closely related to the place or area hiked are told
Sport
Exercises for the Jungmädel test
Trip games

A meeting with the Jungmädel of the village where a break takes place.

B. Example for conducting a field trip

Probably just as important as the first big trip with the HJ or the BDM, travelling to the Rhine, the sea, to the mountains or some other part of our beautiful German homeland, is the day when our Jungmädel go off with their leader for the first time. That the trip is also a nice experience and that it brings the Jungmädel group a step further in their work and their cohesion is the duty of the Jungmädel leader.

General matters:

All Jungmädel present on time and in clean uniforms at the meeting point.

Then line up and count through.

Collect money for train travel or food if this has not been done beforehand. (Pass for the 50 percent discount must be obtained in advance from the JM Untergau (Lower district leader)).

On a day trip, every young girl should get to know a piece of her local homeland and that is why everyone looks at the map together, at the route that is to be hiked.

Planning a day trip:

Morning: Hike to the intended destination. Right at the beginning the leader divides the Jungmädel into small groups of 3 to 4 girls each. During the journey, each of these groups has to pay attention to something specific. And at the end of the journey, they have to report on it. Make it a competition between the groups. Which has the most to tell?

Distribution of tasks:

1. The form in which the home town is laid out is to be determined and why it was built that way. Perhaps the course of a river, a mountain, etc. is the reason. To find this out is part of the task.

2. What does the landscape look like, which the trip leads through? Flat or mountainous, forest or fields, rivers and streams?

3. What are the names of the villages you walked through and those in the immediate vicinity? How may their names have come about? (Legends and stories about the origin of the place names).

4. How are the farms situated?

5. What types of grain and plants can be found in the fields?

6. How many species of trees and shrubs can be counted along the way, and of which do you know the names?

There are still a large number of questions of this kind, and the Jungmädel should be able to report as much as possible.

Lunch time: Break of around 1 ½ hours. The Jungmädel shall rest.

Afternoon: one hour singing, dancing and games. Then the highlight of the trip, the young girls tell of their observations. Using old folk tales and legends can add to this. The whole presentation can also be done in the form of a small competition.

After that it's time to start the journey home.
A last song is to be sung, before the leader dismisses the girls.

Collection of materials for the Jungmädel service for the first year

The following compilation of the educational material for the first Jungmädel year, is for the following types of service:

1. Service instructions
2. Home afternoon
3. Sports afternoon

Divided into quarters of the year.

The training material for the practical Jungmädel work is divided according to its characteristics and not according to quarters of the year, but is listed at the end, for the whole year.

The implementation of the trip depends on the local conditions.

So that there is no strain, every guide has to adhere to the roster below:

(See chart on next page)

	Week 1 **	Week 2	Week 3	Week 4	Week 5
Monday:					
Tuesday:					
Wednesday:	a) service instructions b) practical Jungmädel work: singing	Home afternoon Teaching	a) service instructions b) practical Jungmädel work c) crafts	Home afternoon Teaching	Practical JM work
Thursday:					or
Friday:					
Saturday:*	Sport	Sport	Sport	Sport	Sport
Sunday:	Field trip: lessons about home region, games and songs, Sport				JM Group roll call

* In the country side, due to long distances, this service can be combined with the Wednesday service.

** On one day of the first week collection of old materials. [Recycling]

Educational material for the 1. quarter
(Month April – May – June)

Overview:

I. Service instructions

A. 1. Service instruction

    1. Service as a Jungmädel

    2. Jungmädel test

B. 2. Service instruction

    1. Service Holidays

    2. Service membership fee

C. 3. Service instruction

    1. Uniform in summer

    2. Uniform for sports

D. 4. Service instruction

    1. Where to purchase your uniform and kit?

    2. What do the individual parts look like and how do I wear them?

II. Home afternoon

A. Home afternoon "Our Führer Adolf Hitler"

B. Home afternoon "Our Reichs Youth leader"

III. Sports afternoon

A. Jungmädel gymnastics

B. Movement exercises

C. The rope

D. The ball

A 1. Service instruction

1. The Jungmädel service – See page 17

2. Jungmädel test

After joining the Jungmädel group, within the first half of the first year, the Jungmädel shall show through her service that she wants to become a real Jungmädel, that she can be obedient and follow her leader, that she fits well into the community and be a good comrade to those who are in the Jungmädelschaft with her.

Her physical performance and the will to fulfil every task that the Jungmädelschaft requires, should be proven by participating in the Jungmädel test, which requires the completion of some simple sporting exercises.

The conditions of the Jungmädel test:

Performance
>   60m (197 ft) run in 14 seconds
>   Far jump = 2 metres (6-1/2 feet)
>   Ball throw = 12 meters (39 feet)

Agility
>   Two somersaults' forwards
>   Followed by standing up without using hands

74

B 2. Service instruction

1. Service holidays

The service is determined by the young girl leader. Her orders are always to be obeyed. If a Jungmädel cannot attend a home or the sports afternoon or the trip for any reason, she has to apply for leave with her leader beforehand. If a sudden incident keeps her away from her duties, she has to apologize to her leader at the next opportunity. In the event of illness, she has to apologize for her absence upon her return. If the illness lasts longer than a week, the leader must be informed in the meantime. Before the Jungmädel resumes her service, she has to report to her leader.

If the young girl wants to go on vacation with her parents or visit relatives, she is also to request leave from her leader a week in advance.

If she is not able to take part in any of her service duties, for example swimming due to an ear disease, she must report to a BDM doctor for examination and produce written confirmation. In any case, the Jungmädel leader can request a certificate from her parents or doctor as evidence of the reason for not taking part in the service.

There is no leave of absence from the Jungmädel service due to a momentary disadvantage at school. In special cases, a temporary leave of absence can only be given when changing schools if the Jungmädel has a lot of catching up to do.

2. Membership fees

Starting in May, the membership fee of RM 0.35 per month including accident protection during service is payable. The Jungmädel has to make this contribution, even if it is difficult and means a sacrifice. She needs to know what it is like to give a sacrifice. She shall save the amount from her Reichspfennig, and she should realize that the Hitler Youth only became great through sacrifice. The amount is to be handed over to the Jungmädel leader on time.

The parents of the young girls have already been informed about the reduced contribution service, accident protection, health insurance protection and "Langemark Opferpfennig" (Langemark German War Cemetery Sacrifice a Penny Fundraising Campaign) through the JM service regulation "Der Jungmädeldienst", which they received at the time of admission.

C. 3. Service Instruction

1. The Jungmädel Dress Code

To make the uniformity of our covenant externally recognizable, we all wear the same clothes, our uniform, as an expression of our common will.

As soon as the Jungmädel appears in her service uniform, everyone sees her as a representative of the Jungmädelbund and judges the entire association based on her appearance and demeanour. That is why her uniform must be in perfect order at all times, i.e. her white blouse must always be freshly washed, the dark blue skirt brushed clean, and the shoes must be well polished. It goes without saying that a young girl is impeccably clean and always has neatly combed hair. **No jewelery** is allowed while in uniform.

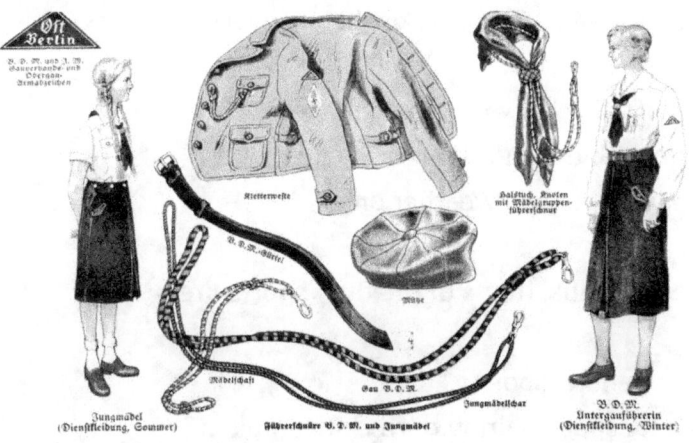

One is in no way superior to one's comrades, if you wear necklaces and bracelets, earrings and star hoops. No small pieces of wooden clogs pinned to the BDM Kletterweste, however cute the pieces. Clothes and knots are not embellished by colorful pendants, and it is just as impossible to wear red hats, green scarves, blue gloves, yellow jackets and light-coloured shoes with the uniform. The unified image of a Jungmädel is immediately disturbed by negligence and disorder. It must be the pride of every Jungmädel, to commence her duties wearing her immaculate dress.

The uniform in summer is consistent of:

Jungmädel cap (only in bad weather)
White Jungmädel blouse with short sleeves and triangle of the Obergau (region)
and HJ metal badge (membership pin)
black neck scarf and light leather knot
blue buttoned Jungmädel skirt (8 buttons)
white turnover socks
brown BDM jacket with triangle of the Obergau
HJ cloth emblem and HJ metal badge
BDM rain cape (bad weather only)

2. The individual items of the duty sports dress

a) for general sports:
     white sports shirt with HJ cloth emblem
     black sports shorts
     black plimsoles with laces
     in cold weather a blue training suit with HJ emblem is to be worn

b) for swimming:
     black BDM swim suit
     white rubber cap, on top
     black headband with HJ emblem

c)   for field trips:
grey lunch bag with grey ties and black leather strip
grey field flask with black leather strip
drinking beaker from aluminium
foldable cutlery

D 4. Service instruction

1. Where do your purchase your service dress and kit?

All parts of the uniform and equipment are bought in the "brown shop", the authorized retailer of the Reichszeugmeisterei (Quartermasters Office).   Shoes can also be bought from authorized shoe stores. These approved shops can be recognized by a sign that has the inscription: "Authorized retailer of the Reichszeugmeisterei, approved sales point of the NSDAP." All correct regulatory items carry an identification tag.

All items that are missing the identification tag are wrong and improper, even if the seller assures that they are correct, and even if they look similar to the legal items of the comrades. If parents, relatives or acquaintances want to give something towards the national uniform, they must be told in advance that only the correct items with the identification tag may be purchased, because non-compliant items without this tag may not be worn.

2. What do the single uniform items look like and how do you wear them!

Jungmädel cap:
It is a dark blue, knitted hat in the shape of the so-called devil's cap. From the front side to the right and left of the tip are 2 white stripes that meet in the middle of the head.

BDM half shoes with laces:
The shoes are made of brown cowhide leather without a toe cap; they have to be laced. On the front part of the shoe 3 G folds are embossed before the lacing. It is forbidden to wear slip-on shoes. New shoes must never be worn on a fieldtrip or in camp, otherwise you will get blisters or even wear your feet out.

Neck scarf and leather knot:
The neck scarf and the leather knot are always worn with the blouse. It is a black triangle scarf that is folded in such a way that it protrudes on the back under the collar of the blouse about 3 fingers wide. The leader will show you how to fold it. The leather knot is of natural brown color; it serves to hold the scarf together.

Gloves:
They are not mandatory, so they can be bought in any store. In any case, they have to be brown gloves. Cuffs must always be worn under the sleeves.

HJ.- Fabric emblem

The HJ fabric badge is worn on the left upper arm of the brown jacket and is sewn vertically above the elbow so that the white border cannot be seen. This is exactly how it is worn on the ski blouse and the blouse of the over suit too. On the sports shirt it sits on the middle of the chest.

The HJ metal badge is worn in the center of the left pocket of the blouse and the jacket.

JM blouse

The blouse is made of white fabric and is a sports blouse with an open collar and short sleeves. There are 2 breast pockets with 2 white buttons each on the front. The buttons are embossed BDM - JM with an oak leaf pattern. The blouse has a fabric strip on the belt line, on the front and back of which 4 white buttons are sewn.

JM skirt

The colour of the JM skirt is dark blue. On the front part of the skirt are 2 diagonally inserted pockets with flaps for buttoning, in the front center of the skirt a fold is incorporated. Eight buttonholes are evenly cut into the waistband, 4 each in the front and back half of the waistband. The two middle button holes are to the right and left of the waistband. The buttons on the waist strip of the blouse are buttoned into these buttonholes.

Triangle of the Obergau (Region)

It is worn on the left sleeve of the young girl's blouse, jacket and in winter also on the ski blouse. On the jacket and the ski blouse it is sewn just above the upper side of the HJ badge, on the white blouse the lower edge of the triangle sits on the sleeve seem of the white blouse. The top is then approximately at the same height of the chest pocket and the name of the Obergau and the Gau (District) association the young girl belongs to is written in white letters.

Jacket

The jacket is made from light brown velvet, single cut with a little collar.

It rests on and is fastened to the side. On the front there are 4 flat, quilted pockets with flaps and through button holes, the brown stone nut buttons are embossed with BDM - JM. A flap for buttons is attached 2 finger widths from the edge of the lower sleeve.

Sports suit

It is well known how the sports shirt, sports trousers and the sports over suit have to fit. It is important to ensure that the correct, dark blue over suit with the identification tag is bought from a "brown store", because there are many exercise suits that comply with the regulations that look similar and are yet wrong. On the outside of the left upper arm, the fabric badge, which is also available in the "brown shop", is worn on the exercise suit, the triangle of the Obergau must not be worn on the over suit. The plimsoles are not mandatory, so any black plimsoles may be worn. There is no need to ask for the tag when shopping. Of course, you are not allowed to go into sports wearing street shoes.

Swim suit

It is made from black bathing fabric and has a round neckline. Please note that the back section has to be cut deeper than the front section. The sleeve holes are also further cut out towards the back.

Bathing cap

Any rubber swimming cap can be worn, as it is not mandatory. When swimming in closed units a black headband with the HJ badge must be worn over the rubber cap. A black triangular scarf can be used for this, the HJ badge is sewn vertically to the middle of the long base side, the tip of the triangle running above the head. The tip of the triangle must lay towards the back of the neck so that the two sides can be knotted together over this point.

Kit for the field trip

The haversack is also mandatory, and it has an identification tag. It is worn by the ties from the right shoulder to the left hip. The aluminium drinking cup and also the cutlery are not mandatory and can be bought in any shop.

II. Home afternoon

The home evening folders of the Reich Youth Leadership bring extensive material for conducting a home afternoon that fall during this period. We limit ourselves to brief information here.

April:

1. Home afternoon – Our leader Adolf Hitler

On April 20, the Führer's birthday, the ten-year-old girls are accepted into the Hitler Youth. As an orientation we bring the young girls closer to the work, life and personality of the Führer.

May

1. Home afternoon – Our Reichs youth leader

The young girl hears about the Reichs Youth Leader, whose life and work are linked to the existence and growth of the Hitler Youth.

III. Sports afternoon

Aim of the first exercise section is for the Jungmädel to pass the initial test and to achieve the medal of the Reich sport competition. The focus is therefore on the athletic exercises: running, jumping and throwing.

Athletics are supplemented by Jungmädel gymnastics, games and Jungmädel dances.

A. Jungmädel gymnastics

The following exercises shall give you inspiration and material for Jungmädel gymnastics for 10-year-olds.

Elephant walk: Walk forwards on all fours, with knees and arms stretched.

Walking like a crab: go into the push up position, butt high into the air and walk sideways, letting hands and feet follow each other

Frog leaps: crouch and hop forward with closed feet, hands on floor for support

Storch stepping: stand upright, lift knee high and stretch leg.

Panther leap: crouch, jump forwards, stretch body as far as possible when leaping and land on hands turned inwards. Who can jump the furthest?

Duck walk: crouch, without using hands as support, move on leg in front of the other, the upper body is moving left and right together with the leg. Expert level: hands tucked under arms, elbows out.

You may think of other animal walks too.

Agility exercises:

Using your right hand, put it behind your back and try and grab your left ankle. Try this standing up, kneeling down and when laying on your belly.

While crouching, left hand on right upper thigh, try and use your right hand to touch the toes on your left foot.

Bank position: Try to lean forward as far as possible without bending your knees or moving your feet.

Knee stand: Turn your upper body that far, that your hands touch the floor next to the tips of your toes.

Supine position. Arms sideways, try to touch your left hand with the tip of your right foot, then keep your arms a little higher and try the same thing.

Supine position. Legs and arms stretched out in the air, wriggling like a beetle lying on its back.

Go biking. In the supine position and in a floating position.

Stand. Grasp your hands in front of your body by holding your hands, climbing and jumping without letting go of your hands.

Bench position or push-up. Release the support by pressing your hands briefly and clap your hands as often as possible.

Further straddle position. Hands grasp the ankles trying to touch the ground with the head. Most of them will do a somersault.

Quadruped. Stretch your legs diagonally upwards as if to transition to the handstand, kick your legs in the air until you fall back into the four-footed position. Who can keep their legs in the air the longest?

Push up. Try to squat with your hands on them and come to the seat.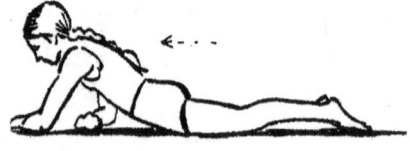

Prone position. Support your forearms and crawl forward.

 Forward bend of the trunk. Hands grasp the ankles from the inside, walk forward without loosening your hands.

Quadruped. Walk forward so that the right arm and the right leg are in front at the same time (pass passage)

Cross legged. Stand up from the cross-legged position without using your hands. Move cross-legged without using your hands or feet.

Kneeling. Put your arms in front of your left next to your feet, up to your kneeling position, and put your right next to your feet. Alternating between kneeling and back to the other side.

Swing. Prone position, hands clasping the foot joints, rocking.

Supine position. Round back, knees bent, arms around the knees, swing with a round back, then swing and stand up.

While standing with your right hand, grasp your right foot from the inside and then extend your leg. Try the same with both legs while sitting.

Supine position. Fold hands over the chest and raise one leg through the hands. Same in
seating position.

With the knee supported, kick your legs back vigorously.

Push-ups alternate between squatting and stretching the legs.

Prone position. Lift your upper body straight up and try to clap your hands as often as possible. Then take your legs and cross them while lifting. Everyone tries to take their hands behind their backs so that one hand is coming from above, over the shoulder and the other coming from below.

Quadruped. With your right hand try to grab the lifted left foot and pull it above your head. Try the same when standing.

Prone position. Cross your arms behind your back, get up as quickly as possible, and then lie down again. You can also do this as a competition.

Supine position. With legs closed, lift over the head until the feet touch the ground.

Walk, run and jump in circles.

Run in a circle, in serpentine lines, in a snail shape, in the shape of an eight.

Run in twos and threes, changing pairs.

Run forwards and backwards, alternating fast and slow on command.

Running with high knee lifts, knocking lower legs onto backside.

Run and step up, and up the steps, so that it becomes a leap.

Horse gallop: with knees bend take one jump after the other, after four small jumps follows one
high jump. With your feet together, you can easily jump around and move around, after every
third (fourth) jump or, on command, conduct a high jump.

During the jump straddle your legs. During the jump, squat the legs.

During the jump keep your knees squat, knees open, and let your hands touch your heels.

Running jumps:
Run with great strides. Step up to the jump, start - and jump.
Also perform all jumps over obstacles.

All the girls gather in a circle and jump sideways alternately to the right and left.

Hop with your legs closed, hop on one leg.

All of these hops and run shapes should be done in long rows, for example, hopping on one leg. With your left hand, take the left foot of the person in front and their shoulder with your right. Then hop forward in a row. Also, as a competition. Run, crouch down on command, leap. Jump up again and stretch your whole body.

Posture Exercises:

This is intended to achieve an upright, straight posture.

Form a circle, grab your hands, stretch your arms out wide, put your shoulder blades close together, head up, then take a few steps forward, let the upper body fall loosely forward, arms to the front.

The same when sitting.

Sit in a circle, put your hands together, put your arms above your head and slowly straighten up again.

Prone position. Head to the middle, hands together, straighten up the upper body, then pull back the arms far, raise your feet and then relax back to the prone position.

Stretch seat. Hands clasped, grasp the clasped hands, lift the upper body, bend forward so that the nose comes to the knee. Straighten out, loosen upright frame and let the upper body fall forwards in a relaxed manner.

Cat hump. Stand on all fours, support your hands so that your fingers are facing each other. Sit back on your feet then push your upper body as far forward as if you would touch the ground with your nose, then make your back round again and get back on your feet.

Crawling. Legs and arms reach out and become stretched with every step forward. When stretching out, keep your upper body as low as possible on the ground. Then also crawl with a hollow back.

Crawl in a long line. Grasp the ankles of the front girl in front of you.

So that these exercises don't get too boring, keep turning them into little games over and repeat over again. Games that have the same value in terms of movement, only that the movement is part of playing.

Example: After crawling, do small relay exercises. 4 - 10 girls each form a team. They kneel one behind the other with grasping the ankles of the person in front. Crawl up to the opposite wall.

Hit the wall, and then run back to the starting place. The team, that has first returned to the original position wins. With this every little exercise can be turned into a game which can be used from time to time to cheer everyone up.

Partner exercises:

Partner exercises lighten our gymnastics and bring much joy to the Jungmädel group. They often require a lot of skill and are designed to work the whole body, to stretch and strengthen and aid to mobility.

Form two circles, one outer, one inner. The outer circle has more girls than the inner one. The inner circle turns to the right; the outer circle turns to the left. On command the inner circle kneels down and the outer circle jumps across. Those who did not find a person to jump over stay outside. Continue to run as before. On command the inner circle starts straddling their legs, the outer circle starts crawling through. The inner circle takes up a quadruple posture; the outer circle crawls through. The inner circle crouches, the outer circle hops over.

The inner circle forms a horse; the outer circle jumps over with straddled legs.

The girls stand up, back-to-back, arms interlinked with each other, sitting down and standing up. Repeat next time without the arms interlinking.

Two girls stand back-to-back; one will try to push the other out the way. (careful no one falls on their back here!)

Two girls stand opposite each other and hold hands, toes closed together, upper body backwards, sitting down and standing up. Also taking turns, meaning one sits, the other stands. Rocking while sitting: the girls sit back-to-back, interlink their arms. One bends forwards and pulls the other over until she is stretched out. Take turns.

Sit. Back-to-back. Arms above the head, legs slightly bend, and swing your arms and bend to the side as far as possible. Also do carts and butter cradles.

Rowing. Two girls sit opposite each other with their legs straddled and hold each other's hands. They take it in turns to bend their upper body forward and backwards. The same also sideways.

High seat above each other. Hold hands, soles of feet touch each other. One tries to push away the other with her feet until her legs are completely stretched out.

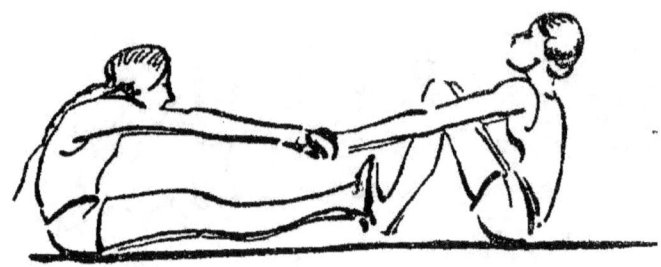

Stand straight, towards each other, hoping alternately on right and left leg moving sideways. Try this one on your own too.

Standing, facing each other, holding hands, turn without letting go. Climb through the locked hands. one starts with the right leg, the other with the left. The legs go over the outside of the grasped hands, then lift the arms up over the head and each one turns around herself without letting the hands go. Repeat from the other side.

B. The rope

Every Jungmädel should own a rope. Old washing lines or twine braided together also works well.

At first hop on the spot and then swing the rope from the back to the front over your head. Do not step on the rope. There is an intermediate skip between each rope skip. Then skip on one leg or from one to the other leg. Always start to skip with the right leg and bounce with the left.

Run forwards – jump over the rope with your right leg, then run left – right, and then jump over the rope with your left leg. Meaning: run (right leg over rope)

> left
>
> right
>
> left (over rope)
>
> right
>
> left and so on

Twist the rope in big turns, arms as high as possible so that the rope does not hit the floor too early. Do the same backwards, and then backwards and forwards alternately.

Skipping with crossed arms

Here you will need to turn the rope twice on one jump, but that is not that easy.

Two Jungmädel swing one rope. Everyone runs underneath the rope without touching it. Then run in pairs or as threes – holding hands of course.

Then run into the rope, jump and run out of the rope.

It is not difficult to skip with a rope. There is an intermediate skip that takes the bounce of the rope skip. Skip as quietly as possible and be as elastic as a rubber ball. Knees and ankles do not stiffen but bounce with each skip.

Run forwards while skipping the rope. Whoever joins in has to run as well.

Next run forwards and backwards. Whoever jumps needs to adjust to the skipping rope.

The clock:

Swing the rope as before.

Everyone jumps into the rope. Raise the number of skips to twelve. If one touches the rope, one of the Jungmädel swinging the rope will take her place. Repeat, jumping into the rope from the other side.

The journey:

Swing the rope as before.

Jump in without mistake, meaning you need to jump in as the rope swing. One follows the other. Whoever misses, takes the place of one of the swingers.

Another game:

Whoever skips the rope need to recite and mimic the following words:

Liesel, Liesel, turn around
Liesel, Liesel, bend about –
Liesel, Liesel, show your shoe -
Liesel, Liesel, how old are you? -

C. Jungmädel athletics

Running, throwing and jumping is independent of expensive exercise equipment. It is important to us that every 10-year-old Jungmädel runs, throws and jumps. It is necessary that every 10-year-old Jungmädel receives a good basic introduction into athletics.

Running:

The Jungmädel is capable of running 60 m (196 feet) in 14 seconds.

1. Short distance run

A distance over 50 to 60 m (164 – 196 feet) is applicable here.

Start: The start is designed to pick up speed from the resting position and to reach the fastest possible running time. Two holes dug into the starting area will support the runner with her start.

The start command is as follows:
"Ready" – "steady" – (pause for 2 seconds) – "fire"!
(or clap your hands)

There is a two second pause between "steady" and "fire". Between "ready" and "steady" there should be a slightly longer pause, to give the runners chance to gather themselves.

99

The way the command is given, is quite often the reason for a bad start. Therefore, it is necessary that the command is well rehearsed. Every Jungmädel and every JM leader candidate must be capable of giving the command in a calm yet forceful manner. The command "ready" should be spoken emphasizing each syllable and not just as a hasty word.

Upon the command "ready", the runner takes up her place at the start and lets herself down on one of her knees. The hands are placed on the start line, shoulder width apart, (thumb and index finger spread out). The arms are stretched. Now the command "steady" will follow. The runner lifts her knee off the ground, the upper body pushes forward, all her body weight rests on her stretched-out arms. The back is in a horizontal position. Both heels are lowered as far as possible. The calf muscles are stretched. In this position, eyes firmly on the running track, the runner now awaits the fire of the start gun or the clapping of hands. Where ever there is no start gun available; the clapping of the hands will indicate the beginning of the race. Upon the "signal", the runner will push herself away from the floor with all her strength using her arms as an aid. If she sets off on the right leg, the right arm will follow, the left one will reach back. The first steps are small, fast and powerful, the upper body pointing forwards and only slowly straightening out during the run.

Before we start running from the starting position, we will train the sequence **using short, tight steps.** The starting foot in front, the other foot is resting on the ball of the foot. Both legs are slightly bend, the upper body is tilting forwards, arms are hanging loosely to either side. Upon the command "steady", the upper body is tilted further forwards. Upon the start sign, a strong push from the back foot and then bending the legs and fast forward to the first step. The heel should be down as far as possible, and one should start with a bounce followed by a strong push and stretch of the take-off leg.

Creating the starting holes

After drawing the start line, you can determine where the front starting hole for the talus is going, and that is a foot's length behind the start line. Now kneel down so that the knee of the back leg is roughly at the ball of the foot of the other. The second starting hole is dug where the toe of the back leg is now. The back surface of the launch pit is bevelled. The starting pit itself is so deep that there is room for at least half of the foot. The foot will be able to push off the ground all the more conveniently and even more forcefully.

Starter and time keeper

The sign to start is given by a starting pistol or by clapping your hands.

This must be done quite evenly.

The girl, who lets her comrades start, places herself behind them. At the other end a time keeper must observe the movements of the runner quite carefully. Upon the command "ready" the latter needs to hold her hands above her head. Upon the command "steady" she will move her arms to the side and then upon the command "go", she will clap her hands. This is the way to communicate between starter and time keeper.

Time keeping requires a little training. If a target band is available, this should be used, for this will lead to more precisions, especially with non-trained time keepers. The target band will be set up at chest hight.

Starter and time keeper should be well versed girls.
Especially in athletics, it is important to conduct precise starts, time keeping and measuring.

2. The relay

The pendulum relay is the only suitable type of relay for the 10-year-old girls. The pendulum is placed into the stretched-out hand of the next runner. Precise change overs should be conducted and continuously trained.

The pendulum relay

With a pendulum relay, the changeover is conducted at a border post. The next runner comes back on the previous one. At the end of the set route the correct amount of runner is positioned behind the

103

border posts, that indicate the set track. The arriving runner carries the relay baton in her right hand and passes it over to the, from her view, left side of the post. Meaning that the baton is not moved to the left hand but passed over from right to right. The approaching runner holds the baton at the bottom end, so that the receiving runner can take it over at the top end. The baton is passed over at shoulder height. Upon approach the arriving runner will of course stretch her hand out as far as possible and pass the baton over into the also stretched out hand of the next runner. A precise changeover will need to be conducted and is to be practiced as often as possible.

3. Long jump
a) In general
A long jump facility can be set up anywhere. It consists of a running track, a beam let into the ground, ca. 15 cm (6") wide, and the jump pit, which is filled with sand that always needs to be soft and needs to be raked. The beam should be chalked or painted white; it must be clearly visible.

All Jungmädel must be capable of jumping a distance of 2 metres (6-1/2 feet).

The long jump is defined by a good run-up and jump-off. The movements can be sectioned as follows:

> running
> jumping
> working while in the air
> landing

b) The run-up

The distance of the run-up is between 20 – 25 metres (65 – 80 feet). In order to hit the beam, one needs to make a mental note of where to run from. The run-up is conducted at speed, which will be increased, with the highest speed being reached about 8 metres (26 ft) before the jump-off beam.

Do not hop or tiptoe just before reaching the beam, this is not conducive to a good jump.

c) The jump-off

The whole sole of the foot touches the beam. Do not overstep!

Take a powerful jump heading forwards and upwards. Doing this you should try and keep your body in the air as long as possible.

Upon landing both legs are thrown forwards, but not too far, for the upper body must not fall backwards. The biggest mistake is a shallow jump-off. Far jump means to jump high from the beam. The force of the run-up moves the body on further.

Measuring the far jump:

The pit is raked after each jump. No tracks from the previous jump must be visible. The imprint that is closest to the beam is marked by inserting a piece of wood or a pencil, measurement is taken from there. The length of the jump is taken up to the beam (edge of the beam). Overstepping the beam makes the jump invalid.

During a competition, every girl takes three jumps. Running over the beam also makes the jump invalid.

4. Throwing (Shot put)

A Jungmädel is capable of throwing the distance of 12 metres (39 feet).

Ball throwing:

Ball: weight 80 -90g, size 20 – 22 cm (baseball size)

Run-up length: any

Measurement: is taken vertically from the launch line

Starting position: The left side of the girl, her throwing arm points in the direction of the throw. The body weight is resting on the right, slightly bend leg, the left leg is loosely stretched, the hip is slightly bent forwards, the upper body veering sideways to the right, the whole body is relaxed and takes a deep swing from the right side.

Upon throwing, the right leg is stretched, and the body weight is moved to the left leg, upper body and pelvic floor turn forwards and upwards and then lastly this is followed by a quick thrust from the arm. If the run-up is not successful, this needs to be practiced. It is a simple series of several steps; speed is only picked up during the last few steps. During this the body only moves and turns to the right (right hander). With the step before last, before the launch, the upper body is completely turned to the right in line with the longitude axis, with the right leg moving forward, so that the body weight, with the upper body turned, is laying above the right leg. Stretching is only conducted when the left leg moves forward.

In order to make it easier for the Jungmädel to learn to throw, a target disc will be used when training the throw for the Jungmädel Achievement Badge. This will exercise the correct core throw. During target practice, one has to slowly increase the distance and aim with precision.

D. Games

1. Running games

Hash or tick. Are known as chasing, catching, tagging or playing ticks. Anyone who has been slapped by the hand of the catcher must continue to catch instead of the catcher.

At the beginning, a place is determined as free zone, i.e. no girl may be caught there. The "being free" can also be achieved in another way, e.g. the girl must not be hit, if she is lying on her stomach or back, not touching the ground with her feet, i.e. climbing up somewhere or crouching down (crouch tick).

The most diverse forms are possible.

This catching game changes if several girls are designated as captors from the beginning, or the girls caught become captors. The game continues until all the girls have been caught.

Ancient Bear. In one corner of the playing field, which can be of any size, is the bear's den. A bear is determined, which all the girls then tease with the following call: "Bear out!" The bear runs out of its cave after the girls and tries to cut them off and to catch them. The captives form a chain with the bear. Only the two girls at the front and at the back have the right to catch someone. The girls that are still free will try and break the chain. If successful the bears have to return to their den. The game continues until there are six to eight bears. Then they are allowed to form two chains. After each third attempt a large bear chain will have to be formed once more. If one of the players oversteps the playing field they will also turn into a bear. The last remaining player is the winner and will be the bear during the next game.

Catching the thief. The set-up is the same than the game "teasing and catching". Meaning two equally strong parties stand opposite each other on a playing field around 30 metres long (100 feet). One side are the thieves, the other the police. A cap or plimsole or any other item is placed on the middle line. Upon command, the first one of each line, thief or cop, run towards the middle. The thief should try to grab the item of the middle line and run back to his fellow thieves; the cop will try to catch the thief. Should she succeed, she will take the thief with her behind her own lines as a prisoner. If the thief however reaches her own line before being caught, the cop will become a prisoner of the thieves and must stand behind their line.

Here it is also possible to set the prisoners free again, it the girl who caught the prisoner, becomes a prisoner herself. Then her prisoner is set free and can return to their own line.

Labyrinth. The girls stand behind each other in several lines, with their arms stretched out to either side, thus forming several paths. Now the cat and mouse game begin. The cat will try and catch the mouse on one of the paths. Should the mouse be in danger, the team leader commands: "Turn right!" The hunt now continues on the newly formed paths. This continues until the cat has caught the mouse. The rows must not be penetrated, and the running direction should be changed quite frequently. A team leader is not necessarily needed; the mouse can issue the commands herself.

Running circle games:

"Come or run!" Everyone forms a circle, arms linked, faces pointing inwards. One girl runs along the outside of the circle, taps one of the girls on the shoulder and shouts "Come!" Both run around the circle and try to get into the empty space. Whoever is left over runs around the circle again and starts the game anew.

A variety would be to let the girls sit in a circle rather than standing. Instead of shouting "Come!" the player could also shout "Run!" in which instance the selected girl would have to run anticlockwise while the player continues her own path.

Dog kennel game.

Positioning: Two circles, one inside the other. The outer circle has more players than the inner circle. The girls in the inner circle remain standing with straddled legs, while the girls of the outer circle run around the outside of the inner circle until a whistle blows. Now every girl will try and find a dog kennel as quickly as possible, below the straddled legs of one of the girls of the inner circle. The girls who have crawled through the straddled legs, will now form the inner circle. Those who did not succeed will have to run again with the new girls. This game can also be varied by using commands such as: "Outer circle, change direction!" or "One whole turn!" or even: "Crouch first, before finding the entrance to the kennel!"

Building bridges

The girls stand in pairs, in a circle and raise their arms, hands touching, building a bridge. A girl that is left over, pick one of the pairs and taps them off, and remains at the empty place, while the girls run around the circle underneath the bridges, setting off in opposite directions. The girls who return first, units with the awaiting girl and forms a new bridge. The other will start the game over again. Varieties are also possible here, like running with a limp, hopping or crawling.

2. Bustling games

Chicken and vulture. One girl plays the vulture, who wants to steal the chicks from mother hen. Mother hen and her chicks stand in one line, behind each other, the chicks with their hands around each other's hips, with the first chick's hands are  around her mother's hips. The vulture must now try to knock off one chick, which mother hen will try to prevent using her arms and hands, stretched out wide. If one chick is knocked off it becomes the vulture. Or in another variant, the chick and all the chicks behind her are classed as caught. The game is finished when all chicks have been caught by the vulture.

Wrestling circles. Form small circles, with a club or a stick (or balls set up as a pyramid) in the middle. The girls have to now try, by means of pushing, pulling or bumping, to get one of the girls to knock the object over. Skilful jumps will have to be done to avoid the object. Whoever bumps into the object, is out. The contest continues until only two girls are left over. Watch these last two fight an exciting battle trying to avoid the object.

Changing places. All girls sit in a circle, with their back to another girl. One girl stands in the middle and upon her command all girls sitting in the inner circle must find themselves a new backrest. As the girl in the middle joins in, one girl will be left over, and the game starts anew. This time it will be the girls from the outer circle that will be changing places. All places should somewhat be marked.

Slipper search. All girls sit tightly together in a circle on the floor. Their knees bend. A slipper or other item of similar size is passed around under the knees, and of course all hands are moving underneath the knees at all times, trying to make it difficult for the girl to try and find the slipper. As the slipper is passed, it may also suddenly change direction. If the girl finds the slipper, she will be joining the circle, the girl with whom she discovered it, will now start the search.

3. Ball games in a circle

Ball hunt. Count off in pairs in an open circle. All No. 1s form one team, all No.2s form another team. There are two balls in this game. At the beginning of the game one ball is with the first girl of team 1. The other ball is opposite her with a girl of team No.2. The hunt will commence upon command. The balls are thrown to the member opposite of the same team, meaning every second girl. The aim of the game is to throw the ball fast and precise, and at the same time overtake the ball of the other party. If one of the parties succeed, they will receive one point. The balls then go back to their original starting point and the game begins again. Points will be counted after the time set at the beginning of the game runs out. The team with the highest score wins.

Hunters ball. The girls in the circle count off in pairs. All girls with the No.1 are the horses, the others are the riders. The riders sit on the back of the girls, who have now crouched on all fours, and are passing a ball. But the horses are being  difficult, bucking and kicking, thus catching the ball is not easy. A minus-point is awarded to the team each time the ball falls to the floor. After 5 to 10 rounds, horses become riders and vice versa. Which party will accumulate the most minus-points?

6-day race. This is normally known as a running game. Here, we also form of two circles with an equal number of girls. A ball will be passed at speed from girl to girl. No girl must be left out. The ball circles for 6 rounds, then the first girl will quickly return it to the middle of the circle, where she took it from at the beginning of the game.

Ball and castle. All girls are lined up in a wide circle around the castle (three poles that have been set up as a triangle). One of the girls' steps into the circle to guard and defend the castle. The girls in the circle will try and hit the castle with a hollow ball, but the guard is alert and stops the ball from hitting the castle by all ways and means. She may do this using, hands, feet, her whole body and at the same time send the ball back to the circle. Whoever hits the castle with the ball, will become the guard. Be aware that you can only throw the ball from outside the circle line.

If we have set up 3 to 5 poles as a castle, the games continue until all poles are laying on the floor and the guard will always have the opportunity to mend her castle, if there is time.

Another, more difficult variant could be that the guard can only stop the ball using a stick.

In this game skillful teamwork is important and will surely achieve more strikes against the castle.

Ball clap. The girls stand in a large circle with one girl in the middle, who shall throw the ball at one of the girls in the circle. But before she throws the ball, she needs to tease the other girl quite severely. This girl must clap her hands once, before she catches the ball. Forgetting to clap hands or clapping before the ball is thrown, is classed as a failure and the girl will have to sit down. She will not be able to participate again until another girl makes a mistake. Not catching the ball is also classed as a mistake.

Variant: All girls who have made a mistake must remain seated until only one girl remains left over, who is then the winner.

Nation ball. This game can be made interesting by allocation names of nations or animals. If there are more than ten girls, several circles will be formed. Every girl chooses the name of a nation or an animal. The game begins after a small ball has been placed in the middle of the circle or into a pit situated in the middle of the circle.

Once all girls have joined hands, the team leader calls out a name, loud and clear. The girl with the name called runs to the middle and picks up the ball. In the meantime, the other girls run off as fast as possible. The minute the girl picks up the ball she shouts: "Stop!" All other girls freeze in their positions. The girl with the ball will then throw the ball at one of the girls. If she succeeds, this girl will take her place, if she misses, she will receive a minus point. The person with the least minus points at the end of the game will be the winner.

4. Ball games and relay:

Travelling ball. As well as simple relays we want to use ball relays during sports lessons. Depending on the number of girls present, we will form two rows with the same number of girls. One ball (medicine ball, hollow ball or a larger rubber ball) will be passed through the rows with as many variants as one can think off. Once the ball has reached the end of the row, it can either be passed back or the last girl running will take it back to its starting position. The party who has returned the ball to its starting positions first is the winner.

Here are some examples: the ball makes its way through the straddled legs of the row. The girls should stand behind each other as close as possible. The last in the row is already prepared to take the ball and run to the front and then passes the ball, starting another relay.

Or: The ball makes its way across the heads of the girls, passed from one hand to the next. No one must be left out. If someone drops the ball, they must fetch it back to continue. Also repeat this game sitting with hand stretched high above the head.

Or: We combine the previous two variants. The ball wanders alternately through the straddled legs or above the head. For this at least one-meter (3 ft) distance must be available between each of the girls.

Or: The ball wanders across the stretched hands of all the girls. The last one takes the ball and crawls back through the straddled legs of her comrades as fast as she can, positions herself in front of the first one and the game begins again.

Or: The ball is passed backwards alternately, once left, once right, winding like a snake.

There a plenty of different variants possible.

Travelling ball in an alley. The girls have formed two rows, standing opposite each other. The distance depends on the ball, the method of throwing and the skilfulness the girls are capable of doing.

All girls have numbers. The girls with the even numbers form one row, the girls with the uneven numbers the other. The ball now wanders down the alley, for 1 to 2 to 3 and so on.

At the beginning of the game both girls at the front of either row have a ball and the game starts on command.

Ball rolling. Two or more parties stand in rows next to each other. The first one of each row rolls the ball to a specific point and back again, before she touches hands with the next girl, who then takes over.

There are plenty of variants to play this relay. To mention one example here: the ball is rolled around an obstacle (tree, bench, table) before it is rolled back to the relay team!!!

Or you use more than one ball at the same time. It makes for even more fun if you use three balls of different sizes (medicine ball, hand ball, throw ball).

Triple ball run. Six or more groups are standing next to each other, each group forming a row. Each group receives three balls (throwing balls). In front of each group, at a distance of 5 metres (16 ft), small circles are drawn on the floor, each of them containing a container (hat, bucket, or even a hole in the ground). Instead of using balls, one can also use stones. Plimsoles would also serve the purpose. To begin with three balls lay next to the first girl of every group. Upon command the first girl takes the first ball and runs to the container to put it down, turns, runs back and fetches the second ball, and then repeats before she gets the third ball. Upon her return, the next girl receives a handshake and must now go and fetch the balls back, meaning she moves around in reverse order. The third girl, once she has received her hand shake, takes the balls back out again. And so on and so forth. Each girl that has completed her run, joins her team at the back of the queue.

The game can be simplified if all three balls are taken out in one run and are brought back in one run. A starting point should be drawn on the floor, so that no one over steps and gains an unwanted advantage.

Order exercises

The following commands are fixed terms used during the work with the Jungmädel:

Command:	Execution:
In line:	All girls step into line next to each other, the first one stands at a greater distance (3 – 4 m) in front of the leader.
In row:	All girls gather behind each other, the first at the correct distance from her leader.
In marching column:	The first three girls stand in front of their leader, the others in rows of three behind them.
Attention:	Is the word we use each time before giving a new command, i.e. attention – turn right – run.
Count:	We do this to establish the strength of our group. This is done in a natural way, without turning heads.

March in lockstep: The leader commands this quietly, only for the first row of girls to be heard. The other girls follow the first row naturally.

Great stop: Is a command we use, when we have arrived at our designated point. This command is also said that quietly, that only the first row of girls can hear this. The other girls close up and stand still.

Left turn, right turn: Every girl takes a quarter of a turn on the spot.

Turn left or right twice (this used to be called "In return" This is a command that is used for marches, especially during sports events, but should be avoided.

Dismiss! The girls go to get changed or go home etc.

Every leader and sports leader must know that us girls do not march. If marching is needed to lead a group of girls orderly along a street, the girls should walk orderly, straight, and without talking to one another and where ever possible they should be singing.

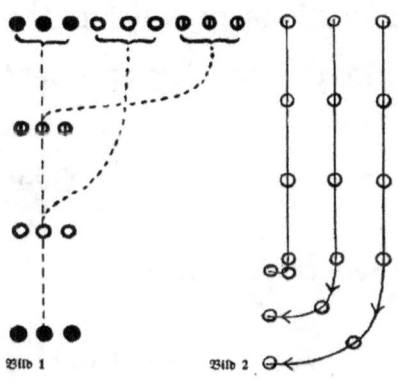

At crossroads it is imperative, that the group turns into the road in a correct manner or even crosses the road. Turning a corner will be done without the military "in return", meaning one will walk in a small turn.

The J.M. leader must take great care that the girls do not walk using the "Pimpfen step". A lot of Jungmädel seem to have the habit of setting their left foot down heavily. This bad habit needs to be erased as well as the rhythmic whistling of some of the J.M. leaders.

Singing while walking is important. The Jungmädel must learn that the front of the column starts the song. Between each verse, a double step must be conducted, and the accentuation of the song always lays on the left foot.

Educational material for the 2. quarter
(Month July – August – September, under consideration of leave)
Overview:

I. Service Instruction

A. 5. Service instruction

Compulsory songs

> 1. German Anthem | Page 185
> 2. Horst Wessel Song | Page 186
> 3. H.J. Song | Page 188

Here one must not only ensure that these songs are sung correctly in text and melody, but it is also down to the J.M. leader to explain the meaning and educate about the origin of these songs. This is especially important for the two national anthems.

B. 6. Service instruction

Appearance of the Jungmädel in her service uniform

1. Question: When do you wear your service uniform?
   Answer: For every service and on every field trip.

2. Question: Are you allowed to wear your uniform at any other occasions?
   Answer: Yes, on all official bank holidays of the Reich, the movement and on very special family occasions.

3. Question: When are you not allowed to wear your uniform?

Answer: I must not wear my uniform at school, unless my
             leader has ordered me to do so; at church, i.e.
             church services or holy celebrations and when
             visiting fairgrounds.

4. Question: Which parts of your uniform may you wear on
              civil occasions?

Answer: On civil occasions I may wear
             the Jungmädel cap
             the white blouse, **without** triangle and badge

             the skirt
             the turnover socks
             the shoes
             the jacker **with** triangle and badge
             the rain cape
             the sports-, swim- and ski wear **without** badge

C. 7. Service instruction

The Greeting

The greeting is always the greeting of the Germans, "Heil Hitler". It is to be executed with precision. The right arm is stretched out during the greeting to eye level. The Jungmädel, whether in uniform or not, uses this greeting to greet friends, family, teachers and comrades.

When in national uniform, the girls, the J.M. leader, the H.J. leader, leaders of the party, the local group and cell leaders, SA leader and local Frauenschafts (National Socialist Women's League) leaders are to be greeted, as well as the BDM girls and Jungmädel. Naturally the Jungmädel greets her comrades too. As the matter of course the Jungmädel always greets first.

Further to this, flags of the movement, the Wehrmacht and flags and banners of the H.J. are to be greeted, as well as standards, displayed on cars. When singing or playing the German anthem or the Horst Wessel song and when reciting the refrain of our H.J. song: "Our flag flies before us" the right arm will also be raised in greeting.

D. 8. Service instruction

The winter dress of the J.M.

For service:

    the Jungmädel cap

    white Jungmädel blouse with short sleeves and triangle of the Obergau

    (black neckerchief and leather knot tie)

    blue, button attachable Jungmädel skirt

    long, mottled brown Stockings (wool stockings)

    brown BDM half shoes, lace-ups

    brown BDM jacket with Obergau triangle and H.J. cloth badge

    BDM rain cape (only if the weather is bad)

    gloves

The look of the individual uniform parts is according to service instruction 3 and should be adhered to.

E. 9. Service instruction

Passes

1. Membership Identification Card

After passing the Jungmädel test, every Jungmädel will receive a membership pass, in which her membership stamps will be fixed, and which she has to bring with her at every meeting.

2. Health pass

Part of the Jungmädel's passes is also the health pass, which the Jungmädel will receive after her admission examination. This pass has to be brought to each meeting, together with her membership pass, and especially to each medical assessment.

Source: https://bdmhistory.com/research-reference/bdm-documents

II. Home afternoon

Summer training: May until October
During the summer, the Jungmädel shall experience nature, the beauty of forest and field.

During these observations the Jungmädel will learn about their closest surroundings and will hear fairy tales, stories and legends of their homeland.

No home evening educational maps are being issued for the months from June until September. Instead, there is a one-off educational map issued for the summer camps under the subject "Living world".

III. Sports afternoon

Aim of this second training section is getting used to the water, water games and learning the breast stroke. During sports exercises athletics will also be continued. J.M. gymnastics, games and singing dances will be added.

The sport disciplines described below can be found in a similar form in the training regulation for the Deutsche Jungvolk D1.

These regulations have been issued with a series of descriptive drawings that will also be suitable for the Jungmädel. The local Jungmädel group leader will be happy to make these training instructions available to the group.

A. Swimming

Every Jungmädel has to learn how to swim.

The set-up of a swimming lesson is the same than the set-up for every other sports lesson. The lesson must not start with too greater performance. The body must first be warmed and loosened up. Strenuous exercise must only be conducted alternately with light exercise.

Albeit the leader may not be able to be in the water all of the time, but she should be amongst her girls from time to time to explain or show them something.

The Jungmädel will be frightened of water to begin with. They will have to get to know and used to it first. They will not start making swimming movements until they have accustomed themselves with the water.

1. Water habituation exercises

These water habituation exercises will be conducted in shallow water, meaning knee to chest deep water.

The girls will enter the water in a long row, holding hands and once in, will form a circle. They will walk to the left and to the right, then run to the left and the right, and then hop in all possible forms. (Alternately from the left leg to the right, with both legs, then gallop and so on). Nearly all forms of walking, running and hopping are also possible in shallow water. The same as leapfrog, hen fights and doing wheelbarrows. All those exercises can also be conducted as relays or other competitions.

The Jungmädels stand in a circle and splash water at each other. They will continue to face the middle of the circle. When ready, splashing can be turned into a water fight, with two groups standing opposite each other that will fight splashing at each other with water.

Next there will be a new exercise: submersing below water. Everyone tries for herself first, and then all will put their head under water together, as a circle, holding hands. Then count off every second one. The girls go down alternately, one group submersing, the other watching how long they can stay down. And vice versa.

B. Diving competition

Some beautiful big stones are to be lifted to the surface. Whoever brings the most stones in with one dive is the winner.

C. Games

Many of the games that are being played on land can also be played in the water. For example:
Catch with one or two hunting. (The one that dives is free)
Black man
Day and night
Come – run! (with all its variations)
The kennel game (a good game for exercising diving)
Cat and mouse
The third one starts
Tug of war
Games using a ball will make the beginner forget their shyness in the water (nation ball or ball hunt)

D. Jumping exercises

Little jumping exercises, like jumping of the lowest step or from a shallow edge should be done straight from the very beginning. If the water is knee deep, the obstacle to jump off should not be higher than 20 cm (8 inches)! It should be a soft jump with knees slightly bend. Here we will adhere to the following

Rule: No one is to be ever pushed into the water. The girls may jump into the water together, in a long row, holding hands, so that one is driving by the courage of the next. They will soon jump of their own accord.

2. Gliding exercises
Once the girls have grown accustomed to the water through water habituation exercises and games, they are being led to exercises that teach them the buoyancy of the water. They will notice

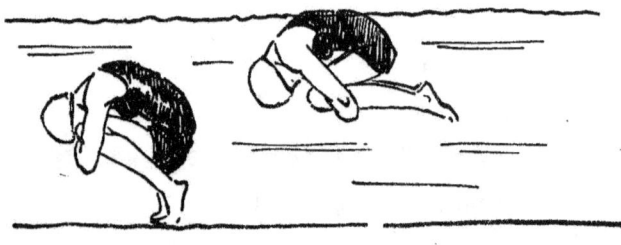

OR

how their body floats in the water. This must include the nose and the ears getting accustomed to the water pressure. Thus, we will increase diving exercises. The girls will all bend down into a crouched position, wrapping their arms around their lower legs and rest their heads on their chests. Taking a deep breath, they should let themselves be carried by the water until they run out of breath.

They will do press-ups in knee-deep water and immerse their head under water. Once in position, they should then let go of their hands, quickly touch their shoulders and eventually rest their hands on their shoulders. This will make them notice that

132

the water carries them, and this because their body with lungs full of air is lighter than water. Once the beginner has learned about the buoyancy of the water, she will be ready to lay her body on top of the water. Soon she will be able to push herself away from the pool edge and after taking a deep breath, she will stretch her body out and make it as long as possible and let her body glide along the water (face under water). Even if this happens just for a second to begin with, she will soon take longer and longer. Competitions could be conducted of who can float the longest or who can drift the furthest.

Once the beginner has mastered this, she will almost already be able to swim.

3. Swimming movements
Dry swimming (exercising the swimming movements on land) is designed to teach the swim movements, especially the arm and leg movements and how they work together. Movements should be smooth and never jerky while also ensuring the correct breathing.

a) Dry swimming
The movement is conducted according to the following time scale: one---two--- and three.

Arm exercise: Arms raised, palms of the hands to the front

To start:	Turning the hands outwards and moving the arms to the side, shoulder high, breathe in. (Ensure that fingers remain together. Water would flow through open fingers, and the hand would not offer any resistance and moving through the water would be more difficult.
Next:	Move your arms towards your chest in a flat curve. Thumb and index finger are touching each other.
And:	Lift arms and return to original position, hands flat forwards. Breathe out.
Leg exercises:	Initial position.
First:	Remain in initial position.
Next:	Lift the right or left knee to the side.
And:	Straddle push off the lifted knee to the side.
Three:	Knock down the extended leg to the basic position. The movements "And Three" must be executed fluently and should not be jerky. Especially the straddle push to the side must be executed calmly, bringing the legs together should however, be conducted vigorously. (A vigorous movement when bringing the legs together displaces the water, this in turn increase the buoyancy and the body moves forward better.)

Altogether it should look like this:

First: Move arms to the side – breathe in

Next: Arms folded in front of chest – at the same time lift
            right or left knee

And: Move arms to the front – breathe out
            Straddle push of the other leg

Three: Knock down the other leg.

When swimming in the water, both knees will be pulled up, straddled and then closed together.

b) In the water

The arm movements will be exercised in such a way that the girls will kneel in the water with the shoulders below the water. The arms will then be stretched out and the arm movement will be trained counting the steps. Pay special attention to the breathing. Breathing is done through the open mouth, not through the nose. The leg exercises will be trained while the girls are doing push-ups under water, or while hanging on to the pool edge, or one girl holds the other by her hands. Pay special attention, that the soles of the feet remain firmly together when the knees are pulled forward. Then the knees open up and are never pulled underneath the abdomen. The legs are moved wide to the side and knocked together when fully stretched. Then both, the arm and the leg movement and exercised while sliding through the water. The girl pushes herself away from the pool edge, head under water, to keep the body gliding through arm and leg movements, she will also be trained with the head out of the water.

The movement of arms and legs working together will be trained the following way: Two girls stand opposite each other and hold hands forming a cradle. A third girl lays on the linked arms of these two, her body in the water. The arm and leg movements are exercised counting the movements down. Pay special attention that the movements are correctly executed as well as to the breathing. Afterwards the movements will be conducted sliding through the water, with the head held above water every now and then.

One day they will be ready to go into the "Deep". Provided they can conduct the correct movements, breathe correctly and feel confident in the shallow water. While in the deep water, these girls should swim close to the edge to start with, one after the other. A pole can be used as an aid, to give the girls something to get hold of should they need to. Better than a pole, is a pole with a ring on the end, that can be pulled around the body of the swimmer, guiding her back to the edge. In time the girls will grow more confident and relaxed and will get braver until one day they will achieve the Reichs swimming certificate 1. For this they must be capable of swimming for 15 minutes and conduct a start jump.

4. Breathing

Swimming means to be able to breathe correctly. Every human can swim, if they breathe correctly. Wrong breathing quickly leads to exhaustion. Breathing when swimming is different to breathing on land. First of all, one must overcome the water pressure pressing on stomach and chest, secondly breathing in is much shorter and more difficult. In addition to this, when swimming, breathing must be abdominal breathing, where as one would use chest breathing when walking or running. Most people find it difficult to swim, because they need to learn to breathe properly first. Wrong breathing leads to fatigue.

When moving the arms exactly back to the surface of the water, slightly sideways, this will cause the upper body and with it the head, to lift out of the water. That is when you need to breathe in, breathing through the mouth.

When stretching the arms forwards again, the head goes back into the water, and precisely when the straddled legs are closed together vigorously, the air will be discarded unter water as one continues to glide.

Educational material for the 3. quarter

(Month October – November – December)

Overview:

A. 10 Service instruction: Function and structure of the Jungmädelbund down to the J.M. group

1. The Jungmädelschaft (Den)
About 10 young girls of a street or a village form the Jungmädelschaft. This Jungmädelschaft is named after the street or village and all the Jungmädelschaften of this street or village are numbered in Arabic numbers.

Example:
Jungmädelschaft 3, Bismarckstraße, or Jungmädelschaft 4 Flechtorf. The Jungmädelschaft is the smallest unit of the Jungmädelbund (Young girls league). The Jungmädelschaft will gather for home and sports afternoons, for trips and camps.

2. The Jungmädelschar (Troop)
A Jungmädelschar is made from 4 Jungmädelschaften, altogether around 40 girls. The Jungmädelschaften in this group are also numbered through in Arabic numbers. The best Jungmädelschaft leader will become leader of the Jungmädelschar.

3. The Jungmädel Gruppe (Group)
The work of the Jungmädelschaft and Jungmädelschar will be brought together in the Jungmädel group. 4 Jungmädelscharen

will make one Jungmädel group, so all in all around 160 Jungmädel. Within the Untergau, these Jungmädel groups will once again be numbered through in Arabic numbers. They will receive their numbers in accordance with the district or locality they stem from.

Example:
Jungmädel group 17/74, Hannover-Linden, or
JM group 20/20 Zeuthen.

The Jungmädel group will display their banner as a sign of their unit. The Jungmädel group is the first administrative group of the Jungmädelbund. All paid membership fees are managed here by the Jungmädel membership administrator, the administrative treasurer.

B. 11. Service instruction: The service ranks of the Jungmädel leadership

The leader of the Jungmädel units are awarded a rank, in conjunction with their service. The following ranks with the following insignia can be found within the Jungmädelbund.

The Jungmädelschaft leader -   wears a red and white cord.

The Jungmädelschar leader -   wears a green cord.

The Jungmädel group leader -   wears a green/white cord.

The Jungmädel Untergau leader -   wears a red cord

The Jungmädel Gau leader   -   wears a black and red cord

In addition to that every Jungmädel must know the name of her Jungmädel Untergau leader.

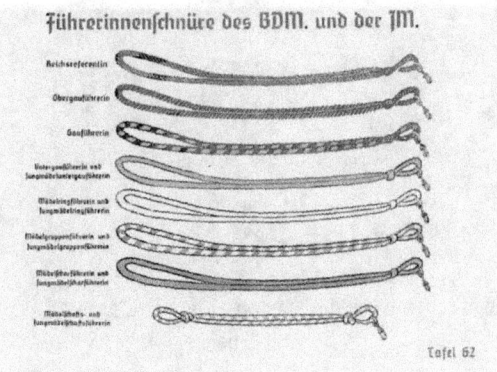

The service dress of the Jungmädel leadership.

Service uniform is to be worn from the **JM Untergau leadership upwards**. An eagle is to be worn on the left-hand side of the dark blue jacket dress. The rank is recognizable from the number of rings around the eagle.

Position:	Rank:	Insignia:
Leader of a JM Untergau	JM group leader	silver eagle without rings
Leader of a JM Untergau	JM ring leader	silver eagle, thin ring
Leader of a JM Untergau	JM Untergau leader	silver eagle, two thin rings
Leader of a JM Untergau	JM Gau leader	silver eagle, one thin, one thick ring

Gruppenführerin   Hauptgruppenführerin (JM. u. M.)   Ringführerin (JM. u. M.)

Bannmädelführerin   Hauptmädelführerin   Gebietsmädelführerin

BDM Reichsreferentin

Source: The Hitler Youth – David Littlejohn M.A.,A.L.A. page 181 © 1988 Agincourt Publishers

C. 12. Service instructions : Flag speeches

1. Legt Eure Hände stolz
um dieser Fahne Schaft
den von der einen Fahne
tragen wir die Kraft.
Laßt diese Fahne hoch
in alle Winde wehen,
denn wie die eine Fahne
müssen wir vor ihr stehen.

1. Put your hands proudly
around this flag stem
for from this one flag
we take our strength.
Raise that flag
let it blow in all the winds
because like that one flag
we stand united before it.

2. Die Herzen sind von Sonne
stark und voll
wir wissen sie zu neuer Tat im
Bunde-
und treten in den Tag zu
dieser Stunde
so, wie uns jeder Morgen
finden soll.

2. The hearts are strong and
filled by the sun
we know them to take us to
new deeds in our league-and
we enter the day at this hour
in a way every morning
should find us

3. Wenn einer von uns müde
wird,
der andere für ihn wacht,
wenn einer zweifeln will,
der andere gläubig lacht,
wenn einer von uns fallen
wird,
der andere steht für zwei;
den jedem Kämpfer gab ein
Gott den Kameraden bei.

3. When one of us gets tired,
the other watches for him,
if someone starts to doubt
the other laughs in faith,
if one of us will fall
the other stands for two,
for God gave to every fighter
a comrade.

145

D.13. Service instructions: Table speeches

Wer jeden Tag nur Kuchen ißt, Pasteten und Kapaunen der weiß ja nie wann Sonntag ist, er kennt nur schlechte Launen. Brot ist der sauerste Verdienst der Welt und heilig, weil es so alltäglich ist, weil es noch immer und zu jeder Frist der Mensch als letztes in den Händen hält.	He, who only eats cake every day, Pies and capons he never knows when Sunday is he only knows bad moods. Bread is the sourest merit in the world and holy because it's so common because it is still and at any time what the person holds in his hands at the end.

May tomorrow bring cheerful weather,
leaving our plates empty and spotless.
Our thanks to the dear sun,
for it brings grain and seed from our earth.

II. Home afternoon

Please take the exact material from the home evening folder of the Reichs youth leadership. Here are just some basic examples.

October

1. Home afternoon – Harvest festival

Harvest festival is a happy day for every farmer. The whole of the German people will celebrate with him on the first Sunday in October. The Führer will speak mid amongst his farmers to the German people in Bückeburg; the German folk will thank the almighty for their harvest.

2. Home afternoon - Sagas of our gods and heroes

We will educate the Jungmädel about our gods and heroes.

November

1. Home afternoon – The 9th November

On the 9th of November 1923, in Munich, in front of the Feldherrnhalle, 16 National Socialists perished as they were shot by government troops. They were the first blood witnesses of the National Socialist movement. Surrounded by the most loyal, the

members of the merit of the blood order, every year on the 9th of November, the Führer marches to the Feldherrnhalle and to the honor temple, where he commemorates those 16 fallen heroes, that are laying here in iron sarcophagus under the open sky.

2. Home afternoon – Once upon a time
The Jungmädel are educated about our German fairy tales, where they will also learn about the fight for the good against the bad and the victory of the light over the dark.

December

1. Home afternoon – A fairy tale performed
The Jungmädel will perform a fairy tale.

2. Home afternoon – Christmas
During the darkest times, we move into the returning light and the new awakening of life at its strongest. This is how we lead the Jungmädel towards Christmas and the winter solstice. We bring fairy tales, stories, verses and songs into the home afternoon during this pre-Christmas time.

III. Sports afternoon

Aim of the third sports training section is to learn somersaults during floor exercises. In additions to this there will be JM gymnastics, games and Jungmädel dances.

A. Floor gymnastics
Floor gymnastics is the answer to the natural urge to move the Jungmädel experiences. Thus, it is a matter of course that some exercises form part of the Jungmädel test and the Jungmädel achievement badge. Floor exercises can easily be carried out anywhere, on a field or in a hall, as long as there is a soft base (mattress, straw, hay or sacks) available. Conducting these exercises, the Jungmädel leader takes on great responsibility, for she must be certain of the aid she needs to provide. Always start with the easiest exercises, before working towards the somersaults that form part of the JM achievement badge.

1. Crawling through and jumping over
Crawling through straddled legs, a window a bench, an alley (several girls crouching on the floor). Jumping across: linked hands, a bench (made by one or more girls), two benches, a trestle.

149

Next, crawling through and jumping over, in conjunction with exercises like prone position in a circle: One starts jumping over, the jumped over one follows straight away, once back in one's original position return to prone position.

2. Somersaults

When doing somersaults, just like with all other exercises in floor gymnastics, aid is of the utmost importance.

a) Aid when doing a somersault:

The person providing the aids kneels to the side of the exercising person and puts her hand into the back of the neck of the trainee, pushes the head of the trainee slightly towards the chest and helps with the turn. All older Jungmädel must train this form of assistance, so they can help their leader during the sports afternoon.

b) Somersault like a roller:

Roll sideways across one shoulder somersault forwards – roly-poly

c) Somersault forwards

Bend knees as deep as possible, round upper body forwards, and pull in head. Chin rests on chest, then put your hands behind the back of the neck and lean the body forwards until it  starts rolling. The body need to remain rolled together until the feet touch the floor again. The somersault and standing up after will be easiest the more momentum and the quicker the movement.

Somersault forwards, from standing with straddled legs.
Somersault, from a start-up run
Somersault, two or three girls together holding hands
Somersault from a start-up, jumping off with both legs

d) Somersault across obstacles

After a short start-up run, jump off with both legs, diagonally forward and high, the arms will catch the body after the jump. Two girls will form an obstacle, either in prone position or crouching down. If this somersault is practiced in a hall, it is imperative that good mats and the necessary aid is available. The trainee is aided from both sides, by the shoulders and if need be, the head of the trainee is pushed against the chest if needed.

151

e) Somersault backwards

Roll backwards over one shoulder
Roll backwards
Roll backwards with straddled legs
Combine both ways of rolling, i.e.
one somersault backwards,
two somersaults' forwards.

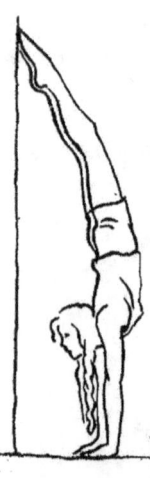

f) Handstand

The main difference between the somersault and a handstand is that when doing a somersault, the whole body is curled together (back round, chest on chin), and doing a handstand it is exactly the opposite, the back is stretched out, hollow, with the head moved back.

The handstand should be practiced in pairs to start with. Two girls are standing opposite each other. One practices; the other provides support. The practicing girl takes momentum, to help her legs get off the ground. The girl that is providing the aid, catches both legs with her arms, by grabbing the trainee round the ankles to steady her. The whole-body weight is now resting on arms and hands.

3. Playful forms of floor gymnastics
a) Wobble snake
Form a row with legs straddled, put your right hand through your legs and grab the left hand of the person behind you. Move forward marching in step! The first girl does a forward somersault and straddles her legs; the next girl rolls between the straddled legs. Hands remain linked! Once everyone is laying on the floor, the last girl stands up and walks with straddled legs across the other girls, pulling them with her.

b) Jump over
One girl sits with straddled legs, hand in the air, chin on chest. The girl behind her grabs her raised hand and jumps over her and finishes off with a somersault. The other girl gets up and the exercise repeats.

c) Tank or double roll
One girl lays on her back, lifts her legs and grabs the ankles of the girl standing behind her. This girl grabs the ankles of the one laying down and rolls through her straddled legs. Note here, that the girl laying down puts her feet on the floor first, before the other rolls. This can also be done with three girls but requires more practice.

d) The middle one rolls

Three girls, the two outer ones look at the middle. The middle one now makes a somersault towards one of the outer ones, the outer one jumps over here, while she is doing this and

then in turn does a somersault in direction of the third girl. This girl in turn jumps over her, followed by a somersault and the game begins anew.

e) Horse racing

One girl kneels on all fours, forming a bench, another girl sits on top of her and holds on to her putting her legs around her tightly. (Do not hold on with your hands!) The horse races as fast as possible, trying to throw the rider off. Who is the best rider?

f) Rolling conveyer (roller)

All girls lay next to each other in prone position. One girl lays across, on her back. The girl is being moved by all girls rolling in one direction in sync.

g) Tug of war using legs

Two girls lay on their back next to each other, left legs touching. They interlink their legs and start tugging until one gives in and is pulled over to the other side. Which girl is the strongest?

h) Push fighting

Two girls sit opposite each other on a flat, slippery surface. They lift their legs, their feet touching each other and now start pushing, trying to move the other out of the way.

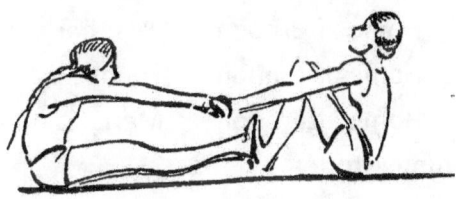

Educational material for the 4. quarter
(Month January – February – March)

Overview:

I. Service Instruction

A. 14. Service instruction: Conduction of personal healthcare (1)

Wash down:
Every day, the whole body is to be washed down thoroughly– do not forget the feet – using soap and water. We use to flannels for this, which can be boiled. One flannel marked with a red edge, for face and upper body, a second, marked with a blue edge for legs and lower body. We also require two towels for drying off. Every girl will have the use of her own personal flannels and towels. If possible, a warm bath is to be taken once a week. If showers are available, the shower time should be 10 mins max with warm water and finished off with a short cold burst.

Hand Care:
Nails are kept short and clean. Cleaning is done with soap and a stiff brush. Dirty nails are a breeding ground for diseases.

Hair Care:
Hair should be brushed, morning, lunchtime and night and platted. Short hair needs to be combed more often.
Hair should be washed every fourteen days in alkaline free soap and dried thereafter in the sun or fresh air. Short hair must always show a neat cut.

Sleep:
While growing up, the Jungmädel needs 10 hours sleeps a night. Even in winter we sleep with the window slightly ajar. The mattress must be firm, so that the spinal column finds firm hold. A mattress topper might keep warm, but it also softens. Day clothes have to be removed during the night. Sleeping in a training suit when on a field trip or camp, is harmful to health and not permitted.

B. 15. Service instruction: Conduction of personal healthcare (2)

Clothing:
Clothing is designed to protect and warm the human being. In summer it is light and airy, to expose the body to enough sun and air. In winter clothing must provide the necessary warmth. When frosty, a woollen hat and woollen gloves are to be worn, as well as a woollen cardigan under the BDM Kletterweste. From 1. October until 1. April woollen stockings are to be worn with the dress. Knee length socks are detrimental to our young girl's health, for they encourage varicose veins.

Sports dress should be light and airy. No daily underwear should be worn under the sports dress.

Oral care:
It is mandatory for every Jungmädel to keep her teeth healthy by:

1. Daily, thorough tooth care:

a) Every morning and especially every evening teeth and gums must be brushed. Daily brushing of teeth and mouthwash must be just as natural as brushing one's hair.

b) The chewing surface of the back teeth needs to be brushed.

c) The toothbrush is set to the gum at an angle and will be moved to and from on the outside and the inside of the gums in direction from the gum to the chewing surface of the teeth.

d) To finish off, swish water between the teeth and press through the oral cavity.

e) Every girl possesses their own tooth brush.

2. Additional care for teeth:

a) Slow, thorough chewing of all food is important

b) Hard baked rye bread, apples and carrots are especially suitable for self-cleaning of teeth.

c) Do not take any fluids while eating.

d) Sticky foods such as white bread, cake and sweets are bad for teeth.

e) Foods that are too hot and too cold damage the tooth enamel.

3. Regular dental check-ups

a) A tooth treated early is easier and almost painless to treat, unlike one that is almost destroyed.

b) Once a tooth starts aching, its nerve structure has already been destroyed to a point where the dentist is only able to repair it by means of large fillings or it may even have to be extracted.

c) Bad teeth can be the reason for a number of other serious ailments, like infections of the jaw bone, illnesses effecting the joints, the heart, the kidneys, the nerves system and the muscles.

d) Thus, we have our teeth checked on a regular basis by a dentist.

C. 16. Service instruction: Compulsory songs

Repeat:
1. The Horst Wessel song
2. The German anthem
3. H.J. song

New songs to learn are:
1. Auf hebt unsere Fahnen | Page 189
2. Nichts kann uns rauben….. | Page 196

D.17. Service instruction: The life of our Führer

Adolf Hitler was born in Braunau am Inn, Austria, on 20. April 1889. His father was a customs officer. He wanted to become a painter of fine arts against the will of his father. He then lost his father when he was 13 and his mother when he was 16. He was alone and went to Vienna, where he had to earn his money under difficult circumstances working in construction. He was impoverished. In spring 1912 Adolf Hitler moved to Munich. In 1914, with the beginning of World War 1 he volunteered his services and fought in France. He had the rank of private and received the Iron Cross first class. He heard about the collapse of the German Reich in 1918 while in a military hospital. He decided to become a politician. He became leader of the NSDAP. On the

9. November 1923 the first 16 men of the movement lost their lives at the Feldherrenhalle Munich. Adolf Hitler was sentenced to 5 years' incarceration. On 30. January 1933 the president of the German Reich, Paul von Hindenburg, asked him to be Reichs chancellor. Thus, he became leader of the German people.

II. Home afternoon

Exact information can be taken from the home evening folders of the Reichs Youth Leadership. The information here is just to give a basic idea of the home afternoon.

January

1. Home afternoon – Walther and Hildegund

The song about Walther and Hildegund tells us how Walther and Hagen wake up as hostages taken by the king of the Huns, how Hagen is able to flee and how Walther becomes the greatest hero in the land of the Huns, without losing his loyalty to his home country. How one day he also decides to flee  together with the king's daughter Hildegund. After many hurdles they finally arrive near the Rhine and start to feel safe, when King Gunther, at whose court Hagen now lives, refuses them to passage across his land, for he wants to take away from them the golden treasure they both have with them. Walther then fights many a brave battle, until Gunther and Hagen, in revenge of their fallen soldiers, take to arms themselves and manage to injure Walther. But they also suffer injuries themselves. This causes them to understand that the gold should not stand in the way of their friendship, and they agree a friendship pact and peace is restored.

2. Home afternoon – Young Siegfried

Siegfried leaves the court of his father and travels the world, seeking adventure and battles to be fought. A bandit living in the woods teaches him the trade of a blacksmith and Siegfried forges himself an incredible sword with which he fights with dragons and encounters several other adventures together with the bravest heroes of the land.

February

1. Home afternoon – Merry tales and other funny stories

This folder contains many funny tales, that show that the winner is always a happy and jovial one, who tackles matters in a good natured and brave manner.

2. Home afternoon – Gudrun

The song about Gudrun is the highest song about loyalty. The people in this heroic song shall serve as an example to the

Jungmädel, how they should follow their life´s path clear and decisive, honest and brave.

March

1. Home afternoon – Dietrich von Bern

Dietrich von Bern is the young son of the King of Amelungen, one of the most daring and bravest heroes of the land. He fights against giants and insidious gnomes. His reputation leads to many a young warrior to travel to the court in Bern, to compete with Dietrich during a battle. Thus, Dietrich finds himself a loyal and brave entourage. One of his  most loyal followers is Hildebrand, his master of arms, one of the strongest is Wittich, son of Wieland. With these men at his side, he wins many a brave battle and he rescues Kühnhild from the king of the gnomes, Laurin.

2. Home afternoon – My service

Looking back over the whole year, this lesson shall summarize everything that forms part of the Jungmädel service and duties.

III. Sports afternoon

The sports afternoons of the fourth quarter will concentrate on obstacle exercises, floor exercises, J.M. gymnastics, with games and Jungmädel dancing also build into the lessons.

The training folder for the first young folk year (Av.DJ.1) contains a series of pictures for the exercises stated below, that may also be used for the Jungmädel service. The young training leader will provide her folder for perusal.

A. Obstacle exercises

In contrast to gymnastics with devices, obstacle exercises do not require certain positions or forms, they do however require confidence, agility, speed, commitment and bravery with every movement. This will be especially required when conducting relays and team competitions, where the commitment of each girl for her team counts especially. Obstacle exercises can be conducted with all girls, no matter if they are talented in sports or not.

Examples:

1. Box set sideways

Roll over the box,
climb over the box,
climb on the box and
jump down, slide on
the box in prone
position and by
setting your hands on

the floor finish off with a somersault kneel on a box and jump off
crouch on a box and jump off jump onto a box after a short run-
up.

2. Box set lengthways

Climb up, run across and jump off,
climb up, crawl across on all fours
and jump off, climb up, and exit
with a somersault forward

3. Stack several boxes behind each other

Run across the boxes,
jump from box to box,
crawl across the boxes,
the same over different
distances or different
heights.

4. Bars placed sideways

Run underneath the bars,
roll over the bars,
climb over the bars,
crawl underneath one bar,
and then climb over the other,
climb over the first bar,
then crawl underneath the other,
climb onto the bars, stand up and jump down (aid)

The very same exercises can also be conducted with the parallel bars set at different heights or with the bars angled off.

5. Bars placed lengthways

Run between the bars,
run underneath the bars,
around the bar supports,
climb onto the bar, stand up
and walk across (aided) and
then jump off,
climb onto the bar and from a
prone position somersault
onto a mat.

6. Bench or floating bench

After a run up jump over,
crawl underneath the bench,
combine both techniques above,
jump onto the bench and then jump off,
walk, crawl, limp, hop and jump over the bench.

7. Hang a bench onto the wall bars

After a run-up, run up the bench and then jump off,
run up the bench, turn around and run back down,
pull yourself up the bench in prone position,
run up the bench, sit down and seat shuffle back down,
with the bench set at an angle, crouch on it with your hand,
set on the bench, increase the performance by moving the
hand further forward.

All these exercises should be used for obstacle relay runs, for the Jungmädel always enjoy a good competition. Everything they have learned during their obstacle exercises can be used here together. This is designed to awaken the competitiveness of the girls. Not one of the girls should try to avoid any of the obstacles or take them in a way not previously described. It is just a matter of honor to compete in an honest way.

B. Forms of relays

1. Line up
In line to build one team. Six cones are placed in front of each team. Distance between the cones is around 3 metres or less.

a) Each girl jumps over each cone, runs back past the row of cones, slaps the next girl's wrist and then the second girl repeats the exercise, and this goes on until the whole team has had their turn. The first team that is back in position has won.
b) Each girl runs in spirals around the cones.
c) Count off teams of the two. The first girl throws the cones over, the second puts them back into their initial position.
d) All girls touch shoulders, forming a long row. The row runs over the cones with straddles legs. If a cone is knocked over, the last of the row needs to put it back. The first row that is back on its original position has won.

It is imperative that all girls return to their original position and stand correctly after each relay. This is a good exercise to train discipline.

2. Relays using the wall bars

The girls are lined up one after the other: The first one runs to the wall bars, climbs up, strikes up at the top, climbs back down and runs back to the team and taps the next girl on the wrist.

The same exercise as above, but this time climb over the top bar.

If the distance between the wall bars and the wall is wide enough, it might be fun to crawl through the gaps, then touch the floor behind the wall bar with one's feet and climb back again.

Now we take a medicine ball and deposit it on the top bar of the wall bars. The next girl has to bring it back down.

3. Relays with bench, table, broomstick or batter chains

The girls are lined up in a double row. The first two grab the broomstick at either end. In front of them, at a distance of 5 to 10 metres (16 – 32 ft) stands a bench, another 10 metres further on a table. The girls run round the table, crawl though it and then jump over the bench and run back to their team. There they hold the broomstick about 10 – 50 cm (3 – 20 inches) off the floor and all the other have to jump over it, which then moves the girls that are holding the broomstick to the back. Now they lift it up, over the heads of the others and work to the front and pass the broomstick to the next set of girls and then join their team at the back. The team that has completed the relay first and stand properly back in position is the winner.

4. Relays with various devices
Line up: Four rows, one in each corner of the hall looking to the middle of the hall. Four devices have been placed in a circle in the middle of the hall (vaulting horse, bars, buck and boxes). Each team is lined up into the direction of one device. On command, the first of each team runs to the middle with her  device and takes all obstacles in a circle until she is back at the first one. She jumps off and runs back to her team, taps the next player on the wrist and so on. The obstacles can be run or jumped over without touching the floor in between.

Devices: buck, mat, rope 1.50 m (4') high, balance beam, horse. All devices at positioned 3 m (9') apart from each other.
A medicine ball is rolled towards the devices, through the legs of the buck, around the mat, picked up and thrown over the rope,

caught on the other side, then climb on the horse with the ball in hand and jump off, run across the balancing bar on all fours, pushing the ball in front of you, then back to the team, passing the ball to the next girl.

Devices: As many parallel bars as possible. Place the bars diagonally to the running direction with all bars at the same height. The girls line up in front in two or three rows. The task: Pull or crawl across the bars until you get to the last one, then get down and crawl back underneath the bars.

If one or two of the devices are missing, one can substitute. Tables, benches and chairs are always useful. The above-mentioned relays require a certain amount of skill, and most certainly confidence and no fear for the devices. At the beginning these exercises should be trained individually, then the degree of difficulty can be raised and several obstacles and be set up next to each other. If there are no devices available at all, one still does not have to refrain from obstacle exercises.

Buck position: The girls themselves can form the obstacles. It does not have to always be a ball made from leather that one jumps over. Instead, the girls can position themselves on the hands and knees, tucking her head in while another girl jumps over everyone.

a) Buck for jumping over.

b) Bench (standing on all fours, for jumping over or crawling under.

c) Bridge (straddle stand for crawling through).

d) Double bridge (two girls stand opposite each other, holding hands) for running under or jumping over.

e) Gateway (two girls stand opposite each other, holding hands, kneeling and hold their arms so these form a hole) for climbing through.

f) a pillar for running around, also doing wavy lines.

5. Circle relays

The girls are lined up in pairs, in a circle, the left shoulder pointing to the middle. All girls run around. Upon command the inner girls jump into a straddle stand, facing the middle. The outer girls quickly crawl through their legs. Who is back in their original position first?

Next the outer girl runs on the inside, the inner girl on the outside. Then add a change and make the inner girls go on her hands and knees and form a bench. The outer girls must jump over. Same doing a leapfrog.

Here also, most fun can be reached, when turning this into a relay competition. You should however watch carefully that every girl sticks to the rules meticulously, that they don't miss an obstacle out or run around it or do anything that involves avoiding the obstacle. That cannot be tolerated, and the girls must be aware of this.

Form several circles. All first girls lay in prone position, facing the middle, the second girl jumps over, than takes up the prone position and the first girl jumps over. Which circle will come first? Here also, one can select from various obstacle forms and thus vary the relays.

Within a circle count off to four. In the middle of the circle is an object (ball, shoe or a pair of track suit trousers). The team leader shouts a number between 1 and 4. Next all number 1 run around the circle, back through their gap into the middle to try and get to the object first. The team who has retrieved the object receives one point. At the end of the game all points are added up. The team with the most points Is the winner. Instead of just running off, there are also other forms that can be chosen, like crawling on all fours, hopping, on one leg, with closed legs and so on.

6. Relays in series

The first runs around the row, taps the second, and while she is running round the row, the first crawls through the straddled legs of the girls to the back and joins them in a straddled position.

The same with jumping over bucks, all girls take up the buck position, one behind the other, at a distance of 2 to 3 m (6 to 9 feet). The same goes for the bench position.

The first of each row takes up a straddled position at a distance of 3 to 4 m (9 – 12 feet) in front of the rest of the row. The second girls crawl from the front crawls around her right leg and then around her left leg, runs back to the girl behind her, taps the next girl who proceeds to do the same. The first row that finishes the course has won. One can vary this by the first runner takes the obstacle and then herself positions as an obstacle and the first obstacle runs to the back of the row. And then the whole matter will become even more lively if the girls perform the following obstacles: bridge, buck or bench.

To make the relays more challenging, more than one obstacle could be put up, i.e. jump over a buck first, then crawl through a high bench, step through a gateway, run around a pillar and back to the back of the row. Another wonderful obstacle is a moving wall. Four to 8 girls stand together, hands touching the floor, where one girl has her legs and the girls to the left and right of her have their heads. The other girls must now, one after the other run across this living wall.

Another lively variant is, when all the girls are obstacles and runners at the same time. The girls form a row standing at a distance of 2 to 3 m (6 – 9 feet) from another. They all kneel down and form a bench, the last girls start and jumps over all the others, the next follows, as they get to the front they kneel back down and form another bench. This continues until all girls have had their turn, and of course, this relay can also be performed with the varying types of obstacles.

So, there are very many ways of making obstacle exercises fun and challenging, even with the easiest of means. Tables, benches and chairs can easily be used as obstacles, just as well as a swinging rope and many other things. Even during floor exercises, new forms often appear, that can very nicely be used in a relay of some sort. All these forms bring a great deal of fun to our girls, for they ooze with liveliness, movement and excitement.

Practical Jungmädel work

(Training material summarized for the whole year)

The following compilation of the material for the first year contains the songs the Jungmädel must learn in her first year:

There are further examples for plays that the ten-year-old Jungmädel should learn using songs and song plays. This will then naturally progress into charades and stand-up games.

For service, there are a few examples for games and suggestions for arts and crafts.

The material of songs for plays and charades stated here can only be an example, it may be extended by each Jungmädel leader as required and of course new games can be thought out!

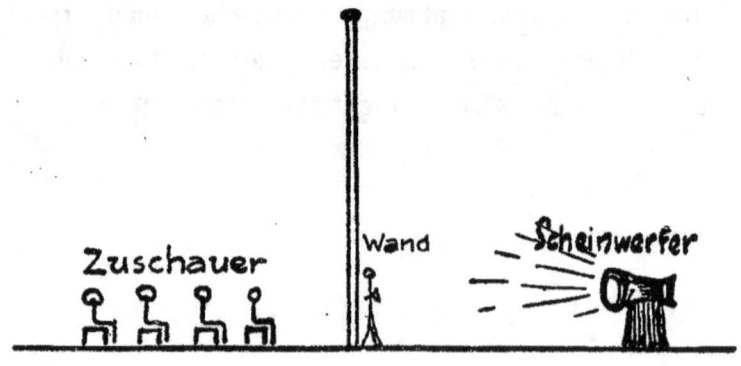

Overview:

A. Parents evening and event ring of the HJ

The ten-year-old Jungmädel shall be involved in at least one parents evening during her first year, where she will be involved in the performing, playing, singing, for she will be much prouder of her service, if she is able to show her parents some of the duties she fulfils. It is desirable to include the participation of the Deutsche Jungvolk. Separate material will be sent to each organization for the arrangement of this evening.

The ten-year-old Jungmädel may also take part in the youth film hours of the HJ as long as these are suitable and comprehendible, including the event ring of the HJ. (Puppet theatre and amateur plays.)

B. The practical Jungmädel service

1. Singing and making music

Singing during a home afternoon, on a field trip or while in camp will contribute to fuse the girls together to a firm community. To begin with singing will be conducted with one voice. It is important to treat the voice box correctly. Over exertion is damaging! Too much singing on dusty roads or in damp weather should be avoided!

The following songs are suitable for the ten-year-old Jungmädel:

Play and dance songs

Craftsmen's songs

Songs about the day

Confessional and celebratory songs will be sung in conjunction with the celebration during the home afternoon and the celebration.

Instrumental groups, as special formations will not be formed until the Jungmädel third year.

Internally, however the Jungmädel group may conduct special service. Flutes, guitars and violins will most likely be available.

The aim of these music groups is to advertise and encourage the uptake of an instrument, music making overall as well as the introduction of German folk music. The connection of the Jungmädel to those German songs, to the music and the plays. She will be happy making music when in a camp and during the celebrations of the Jungmädel group. This will create a fellowship among the girls.

During the first year it is important that all Jungmädel learn a set of songs, that shall become second nature to her. They must analogously fit into the experience of the Jungmädel's first year and should stand in conjunction with home afternoons and field trips. The following compilation maybe extended if the talents and comprehension of the Jungmädel allows.

Instruction for singing

So that our songs become second nature to the Jungmädel, a lively transmission is necessary. Thus, the following should be adhered to:

The Jungmädel leader must know melody and words of the song before she introduces it to the Jungmädel. She must understand the meaning of the song, thus enabling her to be able to do a brief introduction, perhaps even a little personal experience.

The first verse will be sung to the girls, followed by the rest of the text, which is simply read according to its meaning. After this, the Jungmädel learn the first verse by being sung to and repeating parts and whole texts and melody together with the text of the first verse. Any following verses will also be learned by singing. The words will only be written down right at the very end. Writing down will fall away, once the Jungmädel have bought our songbook, "Wir Madel Singen".
The Jungmädel leader will indicate the beginning of the song, the timing when the girls join in and the end of the song by means of appropriate hand signals.

A hand movement signal the preparation to begin the song. This movement expresses: "Achtung! (arm raised), the next movement is "Action!" (the hand moves in tune with the beginning of the song). Now everyone will start to sing t o g e t h e r. The preparatory movement at the beginning also signals the timing of the song and indicates a calm breath before starting.

Once finished, a similar hand movement signals the end of the song.

Attention should also be paid to setting off on the right key. The Jungmädel leader should have that in her ear but may also use a small voice flute.

Loud shouting spoils every song. Always sing quietly, clearly and with precise expression.

2. Songs
a) Throughout the summer half:

> Deutschlandlied
>
> Horst-Wessel-Lied (4 verses)
>
> Vorwärts, vorwärts
>
> Auf hebt unsere Fahnen
>
> Glück auf, Glück auf zur Frühlingsfahrt
>
> Auf, Du junger Wandersmann
>
> Auf, auf zum fröhlichen Jagen
>
> Fort mit den Grillen
>
> Auf, auf ihr Wandersleut
>
> Heißa Kathereinerle
>
> Wir reiten geschwinde

b) Throughout the winter half:

Nichts kann uns rauben
Der Himmel grau
Im Märzen der Bauer
Es blies ein Jäger wohl in sein Horn
Weihnachtszeit kommt nun heran
Bald nun ist Weihnachtszeit
Der Sunnwendmann
Gar fröhlich zu singen, so heben wir an
Nicht lange mehr ist Winter

Wir Jungmädel,

a) Summer Half Year:

Deutschlandlied

a) Sommerhalbjahr:

Deutschlandlied

1. Deutsch=land, Deutschland ü=ber al=les, ü=ber al=les in der Welt, wenn es stets zu Schutz und Trutze brü=der=lich zu=sam=men=hält, von der Maas bis an die Me=mel, von der Etsch bis an den Belt. Deutsch=land, Deutschland ü=ber al=les, ü=ber al=les in der Welt.

2. Deutsche Frauen, deutsche Treue, deutscher Wein und deutscher Sang sollen in der Welt behalten ihren alten schönen Klang, uns zu edler Tat begeistern unser ganzes Leben lang! Deutsche Frauen, deutsche Treue, deutscher Wein und deutscher Sang!

3. Einigkeit und Recht und Freiheit für das deutsche Vaterland, danach laßt uns alle streben brüderlich mit Herz und Hand. Einigkeit und Recht und Freiheit sind des Glückes Unterpfand, blüh im Glanze dieses Glückes. blühe deutsches Vaterland.

Horst Wessel Lied

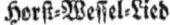

2. Die Straße frei den braunen Bataillonen! Die Straße frei dem Sturmabteilungs-mann! Es schaun aufs Hakenkreuz voll Hoffnung schon Millionen. Der Tag für Freiheit und für Brot bricht an.

3. Zum letztenmal wird nun Appell geblasen! Zum Kampfe steh'n wir alle schon bereit. Bald flattern Hitlerfahnen über allen Straßen, die Knechtschaft dauert nur noch kurze Zeit!

4. Die Fahne hoch! Die Reihen dicht geschlossen! SA. marschiert mit ruhig festem Schritt. Kameraden, die Rotfront und Reaktion erschossen, marschier'n im Geist in unsern Reihen mit.

Horst Wessel Lied

Die Fahne hoch!
Die Reihen fest (dicht/sind) geschlossen!
SA marschiert
Mit ruhig (mutig) festem Schritt
|: Kam'raden, die Rotfront und Reaktion erschossen,
Marschier'n im Geist
In unser'n Reihen mit :|

Die Straße frei
Den braunen Bataillonen
Die Straße frei
Dem Sturmabteilungsmann!
|: Es schau'n aufs Hakenkreuz voll Hoffnung schon Millionen
Der Tag für (der) Freiheit
Und für Brot bricht an :|

Zum letzten Mal
Wird Sturmalarm (/-appell) geblasen!
Zum Kampfe steh'n
Wir alle schon bereit!
|: Schon (bald) flattern Hitlerfahnen über allen Straßen (über
Barrikaden)
Die Knechtschaft dauert
Nur noch kurze Zeit! :|

H.J. Lied

1. Vorwärts! Vorwärts! schmettern die hellen Fanfaren, Vorwärts! Vorwärts! Jugend kennt keine Gefahren. Deutschland, du wirst leuchtend stehn, mögen wir auch untergehn. Ist das Ziel auch noch so hoch, Jugend zwingt es doch!

Unf're Fahne flattert uns voran. In die Zukunft ziehn wir Mann für Mann. Wir marschieren für Hitler durch Nacht und durch Not, mit der Fahne der Jugend für Freiheit und Brot.

Unf're Fahne flattert uns voran. Unf're Fahne ist die neue Zeit. Und die Fahne führt uns in die Ewigkeit! Ja, die Fahne ist mehr als der Tod.

2. Jugend! Jugend! wir sind der Zukunft Soldaten. Jugend! Jugend! Träger der kommenden Taten. Ja, durch unsre Fäuste fällt, wer sich uns entgegenstellt. Jugend! Jugend! wir sind der Zukunft Soldaten. Jugend! Jugend! Träger der kommenden Taten. Führer, wir gehören dir, wir, Kameraden, dir!
Unsre Fahne . . .

Auf hebt unsere Fahnen　　　　　Text: Willy Zorg,

　　　　　　　　　　　　　　　　　Music: Fritz Sotke

2. Soll'n Maschinen wieder schaffend ihre Räder drehn, sollen deutsche Brüder bess're Zeiten sehn, muß unser Streben danach unermüdlich sein, muß ein neues Leben sie für uns befrein.

3. Wir sind heut und morgen, alles, was die Zeit erschafft, ist in uns verborgen, bildet unsere Kraft. Stürmen und Bauen, Kampf und Arbeit unentwegt, wird in uns zum Pfeiler, der die Zukunft trägt.

Worte: Willi Zorg; Weise: Fritz Sotke

Auf, hebt unsre Fahnen In den frischen Morgenwind
Laßt sie weh'n und mahnen die, die müßig sind
Wo Mauern fallen baun sich andre vor uns auf
Doch sie weichen alle unserem Siegeslauf

Solln Maschinen wieder schaffend ihr Räder drehn
Sollen deutsche Brüder bessre Zeiten sehn,
Muß unser Streben danach unermüdlich sein,
Muß ein neues Leben sie für uns befrein

Wir sind heut' und morgen alles, was die Zeit erschafft,
Ist in uns verborgen, bildet unsre Kraft.
Stürmen und Bauen, Kampf und Arbeit unentwegt
Wird in uns zum Pfeiler, der die Zukunft trägt

Glück auf, Glück auf zur Frühlingsfahrt

Glück auf, Glück auf zur Frühlingsfahrt

1. Glück auf, Glück auf zur früh-lingsfahrt, der Wind gibt uns Ge-leit; das Fähn-lein flattert hoch im Blau; 'sift wie-der Wander-zeit.

2. Wie sich im blanken Morgenstrahl der Weg ins Weite schwingt, uns grüßen fernste Berg und Tal, und alles ringsum klingt.

3. Noch blinkt der Tau an Busch und Baum wie lauter Edelstein, die Lerche jauchzt ihr Lied ins Blau und heißt uns fröhlich sein.

"Glück auf, Glück auf zur Frühlingsfahrt,
Wind gibt uns Geleit
Das Fähnlein flattert hoch im Blau
Sift wieder Wanderzeit"

"Good luck, good luck on your spring hike,
Wind guides us
The little flag flutters high in the blue
It's hiking time again!"

Auf, Du junger Wandersmann!

Auf, du junger Wandersmann!

1. Auf, du junger Wandersmann! Jetzo kommt die Zeit heran, die Wanderszeit die gibt uns Freud. Wolln uns auf die Fahrt begeben, das ist unser schönstes Leben; große Wasser, Berg und Tal anzuschauen über all.

2. An dem schönen Donaufluß findet man ja seine Lust und seine Freud auf grüner Heid, wo die Vöglein lieblich singen und die Hirschlein fröhlich springen; dann kommt man vor eine Stadt, wo man gut Arbeit hat.

3. Mancher hinterm Ofen sitzt und gar fein die Ohren spitzt, keine Stund' fürs Haus ist kommen aus; den soll man als G'sell erkennen oder gar ein Meister nennen, der noch nirgends ist gewest, nur gesessen in seim Nest?

4. Mancher hat auf seiner Reis' ausgestanden Müh und Schweiß und Not und Pein, das muß so sein: trägt's Felleisen auf dem Rucken, trägt es über tausend Brucken, bis er kommt nach Innsbruck ein, wo man trinkt Tirolerwein.

5. Morgens wenn der Tag angeht und die Sonn' am Himmel steht so herrlich rot wie Milch und Blut, auf, ihr Brüder, laßt uns reisen, unserm Herrgott Dank erweisen für die fröhlich Wanderzeit, hier und in die Ewigkeit.

Auf, auf zum fröhlichen Jagen

Words: Benjamin Hancke 1724
Song from Kärnten/Bavaria

Auf, auf zum fröhlichen Jag

Worte von Benjamin Hancke 1724
Weise aus Kärnten

1. Auf, auf, zum fröh=li=chen Ja=gen, auf in die grü=ne__ Heid! Es fängt schon an zu ta=gen, es__ ist die schön=ste Zeit. Die__ Vö=gel in den Wäl=dern sind schon vom Schlaf er=wacht und ha=ben auf den Fel=dern das Mor=gen=lied voll = bracht. Tri=di = he = jo di = he = jo di he=di he=di = o tri=di=o, he=jo di he=jo di tri=di=o tri=di = o.

2. Frühmorgens als der Jäger in grünen Walde kam, da sah er mit Vergnügen das schöne Wildpret an. Die Gamslein, Paar und Paare, sie kommen von weit her, die Rehe und das Hirschlein, das schöne Wildpret schwer. Tridihejo . . . .

3. Das edle Jägerleben vergnüget meine Brust, dem Wilde nachzustreifen ist meine höchste Lust. Wir laden unsre Büchsen mit Pulver und mit Blei; wir führn das schönste Leben, im Walde sein wir frei. Tridihejo . . . .

Fort mit den Grillen

After a folk song from Thuringia

Text editing: Fritz Jöde

Fort mit den Grillen!

Nach einem thüringischen Volksliede
Textbearbeitung von Fritz Jöde

1. Fort mit den Gril-len, fort mit den Sor-gen, lu-stig ist das Wan-der-blut. Ja, wir_ müs-sen in die Welt hin-ein_ fah-ren, ha-ben im-mer fro-hen Mut. ha-ben immer fro-hen Mut.

2. Drum, liebe Eltern, seid nicht betrübet, weil die schöne Zeit ist aus; denn mein Berliner, der ist schon geschnüret, und morgen geht's zum Tor hinaus.

3. Drum, liebes Schätzel, sei nicht betrübet, daß ich von dir scheiden muß. Haben einander so treulich geliebet, gib mir einen Abschiedskuß.

Auf, auf, ihr Wandersleut

1. Auf, auf, ihr Wanders-leut, zum Wandern kommt die Zeit! Tut euch nicht lang ver-wei-len, in Got-tes Na-men rei-sen! Das Glück das lau-fet im-mer-fort an ei-nen an-dern Ort.

2. Ihr liebsten Eltern mein, ich will euch dankbar sein; die ihr mir habt gegeben von Gott ein langes Leben, so gebet mir gleich einer Speis' den Segen auf die Reis'.

5. Der Tau vom Himmel fällt, hell wird das Firmament. Die Vöglein in der Höhe, wenn sie vom Schlaf aufstehen, da singen sie mir zu meiner Freud': lebt wohl, ihr Wandersleut'!

Heißa Kathreinerle   Aus dem Elſaß

1. Hei = ßa, Kath = rei = ner=le, ſchnür dir die Schuh,
ſchürz dir dein Rök=le=le, gönn dir kein Ruh.

Di = dl, du = dl, da = dl, ſchrum, ſchrum, ſchrum, geht ſchon der

Hop=ſer rum; hei=ßa, Kath = rei = ner=le, friſch im=mer = zu!

2. Dreh wie ein Rädele flink dich im Tanz! Fliegen die Zöpfele, wirbelt der Kranz.
Didl, dudl, dadl, ſchrum, ſchrum, ſchrum. Luſtig im Kreis herum dreh dich, mein Mädel,
im feſtlichen Glanz.

3. Heute heißt's luſtig ſein, morgen iſt's aus! Sinket der Lichter Schein, gehn wir nach
Haus. Didl, dudl, dadl, ſchrum, ſchrum, ſchrum. Morgen mit viel Gebrumm fegt die
Frau Wirtin den Tanzboden aus.

Wir reiten geschwind durch Feld und Wald

Wir reiten geschwinde durch Feld und Wald

1. Wir reiten geschwinde durch Feld und Wald, wir reiten bergab und berg-
auf. Und fällt wer vom Pferde, so fällt er gelinde und
klettert behend wieder auf. Es geht über Stock und Stein, wir
geben dem Rosse die Zügel und reiten im Sonnenschein so
schnell, als hätten wir Flügel. Heißa, hußa, über
Stock und über Stein. Heißa, hußa und in den Stall hinein!

b). Winter Half Year
Nichts kann uns rauben

b) Winterhalbjahr

Nichts kann uns rauben ...

1. Nichts kann uns rau=ben Lie = be und Glau=ben zu un=ſerm Land; es zu er=hal=ten und zu ge=ſtal= ten, ſind wir ge=ſandt.

2. Mögen wir ſterben, unſeren Erben gilt dann die Pflicht: Es zu erhalten und zu ge=ſtalten: Deutſchland ſtirbt nicht.

Der Himmel grau   Text and melody: Werner Altendorf

Der Himmel grau   Worte und Weiſe von Werner Altendorf

1. Der Him = mel grau und die Er = de braun, da ſchrit=ten die Männer zum Stur=me, und die Glok=ke klang und die Glok=ke ſang ih=ren letz = ten Gruß vom Tur = me.

2. Die Nacht war ſchwarz und die Flamme rot, da ſtritten ſie um die Fahne, da kam der Tod, der ſtreckte ſie auf die Fahne.

3. Und die war rot, und die war weiß, und das Zeichen ſchwarz in der Mitten. Noch einmal grüßten die Lippen leis — ſie ſtarben, wie ſie geſtritten.

4. Der Himmel blau und die Erde braun, eure Gräber und Kreuze, die mahnen. Und wieder vom Turm klingt die Glocke Sturm, nun tragen wir eure Fahnen'

Aus: Werner Altendorf: „Ein junges Volk ſteht auf." Ludwig Voggenreiter Verlag, Potsdam.

196

Bauernlied

From Moravia

Text edit: Walter Hensel

Bauernlied

Aus Nordmähren

Textfassung von Walther Hensel

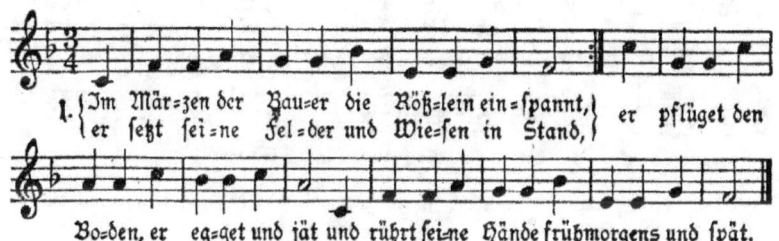

1. Im Mär-zen der Bau-er die Röß-lein ein-spannt,
er setzt sei-ne Fel-der und Wie-sen in Stand,
er pflüget den Bo-den, er eg-get und jät und rührt sei-ne Hände frühmorgens und spät.

2. Die Bäurin, die Mägde, sie dürfen nicht ruhn; sie haben im Haus und im Garten zu tun: sie graben und rechen und singen ein Lied, sie freun sich, wenn alles schön grünet und blüht.

3. So geht unter Arbeit das Frühjahr vorbei, da erntet der Bauer das duftende Heu; er mäht das Getreide, dann drischt er es aus: im Winter da gibt es manch fröhlichen Schmaus.

Mit Genehmigung des Bärenreiter Verlages, Kassel.

Es blies ein Jäger

Es blies ein Jäger

1. Es blies ein Jäger wohl in sein Horn,— wohl in sein Horn; und
2. Sollt denn mein Blasen ver-lo-ren sein,— ver-lo-ren sein? Viel

al-les was er blus, das war ver-lorn,— das war ver-lorn. Hal-li-a-
lieber möcht ich gar kein Jä-ger sein,— kein Jä-ger sein. Hal-li-a-

hus-sas-sah, ti-ra-la-la und al-les was er blus, das war ver-lorn.
hus-sas-sah, ti-ra-la-la viel lieber möcht ich gar kein Jä-ger sein!

3. Er warf sein Netz wohl übern Strauch, da sprang ein schwarzbraunes Mädel heraus.
4. „Ach, schwarzbraunes Mädel, entspring mir nicht! Ich habe große Hunde, die holen dich."
5. „Deine großen Hunde, die fürcht' ich nicht, sie kennen meine hohen, weiten Sprünge nicht."
6. „Deine hohen, weiten Sprünge, die kennen sie wohl, sie wissen, daß du heute noch sterben sollst."

7. „Und sterb ich denn, so bin ich tot, begräbt man mich unter Rosen rot."
8. „Wohl unter die Rosen, wohl unter den Klee, darunter vergeh' ich nimmermeh'."
9. Er warf ihr sein Netz wohl über den Leib, da ward sie des jungfrischen Jägers Weib.

Weihnachtszeit kommt nun heran
Words: Carola Wilke,
Music: Hans Helmut

2. Mond steht aus dem Wolkentor: „Ist es noch nicht Zeit?" Ruprecht, spann die Schimmel an, daß Frau Holle reisen kann; ihre Fahrt ist weit.

3. Pack dir Heu und Häcksel ein, ihr müßt lange fahren. Ruprecht, zünd die Lichtlein an, daß Frau Holle sehen kann, ob wir fleißig waren.

4. Ist das Säcklein leer gemacht bis zum letzten Rest, Ruprecht, blas die Wolken an, daß Frau Holle singen kann uns zum frohen Fest.

Worte: Carola Wilke; Weise: Hans Helmut

Aus: „Tut auf das Tor". Verlag Georg Kellmeyer, Wolfenbüttel.

Bald nun ist Weihnachtszeit
Words: Carola Wilke,
Music: Hans Helmut

2. Horch nur, der Alte klopft draußen ans Tor: mit seinem Schimmel, so steht er davor.

3. Leg ich dem Schimmelchen Heu vor das Haus, packt gleich der Ruprecht den großen Sack aus.

Worte: Carola Wilke; Weise: Hans Helmut

Aus: „Tut auf das Tor". Verlag Georg Kellmeyer, Wolfenbüttel.

Both songs are from the book „Tut auf das Tor" published by Georg Kellmeyer, Wolfenbüttel.

Der Sunnwendmann   Text: Martin
Greif, Music: Ilse Lang

2. „Der Sunnwendmann, wie zieht er ein?" Auf leuchtendem Schimmel wie die Sonne am Himmel voll spiegelndem Schein, so zieht er ein.

3. „Der Sunnwendmann, was bringt er mit?" Gar köstliche Gaben für Mädchen und Knaben, die guter Sitt'; das bringt er mit.

4. „Der Sunnwendmann, wie teilt er's aus?" Er legt sie verstohlen, wo leicht sie zu holen, ans Fenster, vors Haus, so teilt er's aus.

Worte: Martin Greif; Weise: Ilse Lang

aus: „Tut auf das Tor". Verlag Georg Kellmeyer, Wolfenbüttel.

Song from the book „Tut auf das Tor" published by Georg Kellmeyer, Wolfenbüttel.

Gar fröhlich zu singen

Gar fröhlich zu singen

1. Gar fröh-lich zu sin-gen so he-ben wir an.

Was wollt ihr uns brin-gen zum neu-en Jahr?

1. Chor (Wiederholung beide Chöre)

Viel Kampf, Heil und Se-gen und Ar-beit für-wahr.

Nicht lange mehr ist Winter

Nicht lange mehr ist Winter

1. Nicht lan-ge mehr ist Win-ter, schon glänzt der Son-ne Schein, dann kehrt mit neu-en Lie-dern der früh-ling bei uns ein. Im fel-de singt die Ler-che, der Kuckuck ruft im Hain: Kuk-kuck, Kuckuck, da wollen wir uns freun.

200

3. Games and plays

Games and plays form a big part of the JM work. May it be the performing of songs or the connection between song and dance within a sung-through play or later on the fairy tale plays.

By playing games the Jungmädel is enticed to observe. She learns to think of herself into the material in a natural way, if she has to perform it. She receives clear tasks that she has to solve together with the others, and at the same time she can let her imagination run free.

Performing songs

a) The most natural way to learn to perform is by using a song. As soon as the Jungmädel have learned the words and are able to sing the song, they already perform this in their mind. The next step towards a performance play is only small.

Example: Es wollt ein Schneider wandern

1. Es wollt ein Schneider wan-dern am Montag in __ der Früh;
be = geg = net ihm der Teu = fel, hat we = der Strümpf noch

Schuh. „He, he, du Schnei=der = g'fell! Du mußt mit mir in

d'Höll, du mußt uns Teu=fel klei=den, es ge=he wie es wöll."

2. Sobald der Schneider in die Höll nein kam, nahm er sein Ellenstab, er schlug den Teufeln die Buckel voll, die Höll wohl auf und ab. „He, he, du Schneiderg'jell, mußt wieder aus der Höll, wir brauchen nicht das Messen, es gehe, wie es woll."

3 Nachdem er all gemessen hat, nahm er sein lange Scher und stutzt den Teufeln b' Schwänzeln ab, sie hupften hin und her. „He, he, du Schneiderg'jell, pack dich nur aus der Höll! Wir brauchen nicht das Stutzen, es gehe, wie es wöll."

4. Da zog er's Bügeleisen raus und warf's in Höllenfeuer; er strich den Teufeln die Falten aus, sie schrien ungeheuer. „He, he, du Schneiderg'jell, pack dich nur aus der Höll: Wir brauchen nicht das Bügeln, es gehe, wie es wöll."

5. Er nahm den Pfriemen aus dem Sack und stach sie in die Köpf, er jagt: „Halt still, ich bin schon da! So setzt man bei uns die Knöpf." „He, he, du Schneiderg'jell, pack dich nur aus der Höll. Wir brauchen keine Kleider, es gehe, wie es wöll."

6 Drauf nahm er Nadel und Fingerhut und fing zu nähen an; er näht den Teufeln die Nasen zu, so eng er immer kann. „He, he, du Schneiderg'jell, pack dich nur aus der Höll! Wir können nimmer schnaufen, es gehe, wie es wöll."

7. Nach diesem kam der Luzifer und jagt: „Es ist ein Graus! Kein Teufel hat kein Wedel mehr, jagt ihn zur Höll hinaus!" „He, he, du Schneiderg'jell, pack dich nur aus der Höll! Wir brauchen keinen Schneider. Es geht halt, wie es wöll."

8. Nachdem er nun hat aufgepackt, da ward ihm erst recht wohl, er hüpft und springet unverzagt, lacht sich den Buckel voll; ging eilends aus der Höll und blieb ein Schneiderg'jell, drum holt der Teufel kein Schneider mehr, es gehe, wie es wöll.

Es wollt ein Schneider wandern . . . .

Es kommt darauf an, die beiden Gestalten des Liedes deutlich darzustellen. Der Schneider spaziert fröhlich daher, bis ihm plötzlich der Teufel begegnet. Schwarz, hinkefuß und vielleicht auch Hörner bezeichnen ihn als den Bösen, der den Schneider erbarmungslos mitzerren will. Dann muß das Handwerkszeug des Schneiders durch entsprechende Bewegungen und Gesichtsausdruck dargestellt werden. Hier bieten sich reiche Möglichkeiten, und die Phantasie hat freien Lauf. Der Schmerz der Teufel, die der Schneider auf seine Weise mißhandelt, muß deutlich zum Ausdruck kommen. Zum Schluß wird der Triumph des Schneiders und die Empörung des Luzifer den Höhepunkt bilden.

Es wollt ein Schneider wandern

Es wollt ein Schneider wandern,
Am Montag in der Fruh,
Begegnet ihm der Teufel,
Hat weder Strümpf noch Schuh':
He, he, du Schneiderg'sell,
Du mußt mit mir in die Höll,
Du mußt uns Teufel kleiden,
Es gehe wie es wöll.

2. Sobald der Schneider in die Höll kam,
Nahm er seinen Ehlenstab,
Er schlug den Teuflen Buckel voll,
Die Hölle auf und ab:
He, he, du Schneidergesell,
Mußt wieder aus der Höll,
Wir brauchen nicht zu messen;
Es gehe wie es wöll.

3. Nachdem er all gemessen hat,
Nahm er seine lange Scheer
Und stuzt den Teuflen d' Schwänzlein ab
Sie hüpfen hin und her.
He, he du Schneiderg'sell,
Pack dich nur aus der Höll,
Wir brauchen nicht das Stuzen,
Es gehe wie es wöll.

4. Da zog er's Bügeleisen raus,
Und warf es in das Feuer,
Er streicht den Teuflen die Falten aus,
Sie schrieen ungeheuer:
He, he du Schneiderg'sell,

Geh du nur aus der Höll,
Wir brauchen nicht zu bügeln,
Es gehe wie es wöll.

5. Er nahm den Pfriemen aus dem Sack,
   Und stach sie in die Köpf,
Er sagt, halt still, ich bin schon da,
So sezt man bei uns Knöpf:
He, he, du Schneiderg'sell,
Geh einmal aus der Höll,
Wir brauchen nicht zu kleiden,
Es geh nun wie es wöll.

6. Drauf nahm er Nadl und Fingerhut,
   Und fängt zu stechen an,
Er flickt den Teufeln die Naslöcher zu.
So eng er immer kan:
He, he, du Schneidergesell,
Pack dich nur aus der Höll,
Wir können nimmer riechen,
Es geh nun wie es wöll.

7. Darauf fängt er zu schneiden an,
   Das Ding hat ziemlich brennt,
Er hat den Teuflen mit Gewalt
Die Ohrlappen aufgetrennt:
He, he, du Schneiderg'sell,
Marschir nur aus der Höll,
Sonst brauchen wir den Bader,
Es geh nun wie es wöll.

Es wollt ein Schneider wandern ……

Here it is important to perform the two characters of the song properly. The tailor is wandering around quite happily until he meets the devil. Black clothes, a club foot and maybe even some horns will show him as an evil character, who is set into dragging the tailor along with him. The tools the tailor uses should be performed by using the appropriate hand movements and maybe even facial expressions. There are plenty of possibilities here and the imagination should run free. The pain the devil causes the tailor must be expressed clearly, and of course at the end the triumph the tailor has the indignation of Lucifer.

Der Faltrock

Folk Song from the Bergisches Land according to Erk.-Böhme III

Text edit: Friedrich Berg

Der Faltrock

Weise aus dem Bergischen Land
Nach Erk-Böhme III

Vorsängerin: 1. Es ließ sich ein Bau=er ein Falt=rock schneidn, es ließ sich ein

Vorsängerin: Bau=er ein Falt=rock schneidn, von sie=ben=zehn El=len, von

Vorsängerin: sie=ben=zehn El=len ließ er sich ihn schneidn, ließ er sich ihn schneidn.

2. Und als nun der Faltrock fertig war, da ging er, da stand er bei Lieschen im Gras.
3. „O Lieschen, mein Lieschen, sage mir, wie wird er mich kleiden der Faltrock mein?"
4. „Und soll ich's dir sagen, er steht dir nit, der Faltrock hat unten und oben ein Schwipp"
5. „Hat der Faltrock unten und oben ein Schwipp, dann soll ihn bezahlen der Schneider Wipp."
6. O Schneider, du Schneider, sage mir, du hast ihn verdorben den Faltrock mein."
7. „Und hab ich verdorben den Faltrock dein, hab ich ihn verdorben im Mondenschein."
8. „Und hast ihn verdorben im Mondenschein, dann sollst ihn bezahlen im Sonnenschein'"
9. „Und soll ich bezahlen im Sonnenschein, dann möcht der Teufel dein Schneider sein'"

Textbearbeitung Friedrich Berg.

Die Vögel wollten Hochzeit halten

Die Vögel wollten Hochzeit halten

1. Die Vögel wollten Hochzeit halten in dem grünen Walde. Biberallala usw.

2. Die Nachtigall sehr elegant, das war der Musje Bräutigam.

3. Die Amsel war die Braute, trug einen Kranz von Rauten.

4. Die Lerche, die Lerche, die führt die Braut zur Kerche.

5. Der Auerhahn, der Auerhahn, das war der würd'ge Herr Kaplan.

6. Die Meise, die Meise, die singt die Kyrieleise.

7. Der Wiedehopf, der Wiedehopf, der schenkt der Braut einen Blumentopf.

8. Der Spatz, der kocht das Hochzeitsmahl, verzehrt die schönsten Bissen all.

9. Die Anten und die Ganten, das war'n die Musikanten.

10. Der Pfau mit seinem stolzen Schwanz, der führt die Braut zum ersten Tanz.

11. Der Kiebitz, der Kiebitz, der macht so manchen losen Witz.

12. Brautmutter war die Eule, nahm Abschied mit Geheule.

13. Nun ist die Vogelhochzeit aus, und alle Vögel fliegen nach Haus.

Wir sind zwei Musikanten

Wir sind zwei Musikanten

1. Wir sind zwei Musi = kan = ten und komm'n aus Schwaben = land, wir sind zwei Musi = kann=ten und komm'n aus Schwaben=land. Wir kön=nen spie = len Di = o = Di = o = Di = o = lin, wir kön=nen spie = len Baß, Di=ol und Flöt'. Und wir könn'n tanzen hopsas=sa, hop=sas=sa, hop=sas=sa, und wir könn'n tan=zen hopsas=sa, hop = sas = sa.

Vorstehende Lieder und Weisen sind dem BdM.-Liederbuch „Wir Mädel singen" entnommen.

Above songs have been taken from the BDM Song book "Wir Mädel Singen".

4. Singing plays

The song plays usually follow already prescribed forms. The base form is usually the circle. All the happenings take place here. This means that all Jungmädel are included.

Examples: Es gingen zwei Alte wandern….
             Nasses Gras….
             Es regnet auf der Brücke….
             Widewitt mein Mann ist kommen……
             Der Spielmann……

Performance:
Es gingen zwei Alte wandern
Source: „So zum Tanze führ ich dich" by Otto Schmidt

Ausführung:

Es gingen zwei Alte wandern

Quellenangabe: „So zum Tanze führ ich dich", von Otto Schmidt.

1. Es gin=gen zwei Al=te wan=dern, fim=val=le=ral=le=ra, la=la, die

(4 mal wiederholen jedes= mal mit neuem Text).

schal=ten eins des an = der fim = val=le=ral = la = ra.

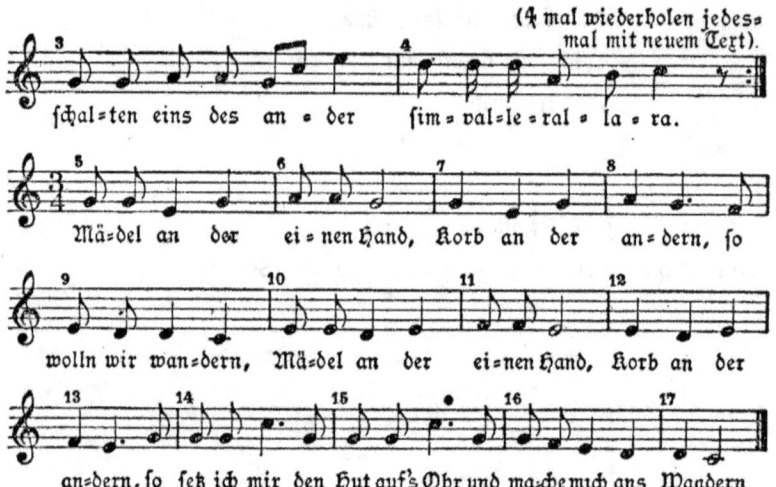

Mä=del an der ei = nen Hand, Korb an der an=dern, so wolln wir wan=dern, Mä=del an der ei=nen Hand, Korb an der an=dern, so setz ich mir den Hut auf's Ohr und ma=che mich ans Wandern.

Es gingen zwei Alte wandern, fimvalleralleralala,
die schalten eins das ander fimvalleralleralala.

Sie stritten um hundert Gulden, fimvalleralleralala,
und hatten nichts als Schulden fimvalleralleralala.

Den Korb will ich dir schenken, fimvalleralleralala,
an eine andere denken fimvallerallera.

Die Hand will ich dir geben, fimvalleralleralala,
bleib du mir treu fürs Leben fimvallerallera.

Mädel an der einen Hand,
Korb an der andern,
so wolln wir wandern.
So setz ich mir den Hut auf's Ohr
und mache mich ans Wandern.

Pace	Form	Movement
1 – 4	circle	All girls form a circle, step movement to the left. Inside the circle walks a pair, arm in arm in opposite direction. This pair accompanies the wording with appropriate movement.
1 – 2 repeat	wave off	
1 – 4	choose	"Den Korb will ich Dir…. "The couple shows this with the appropriate movements.
5 – 8	step over	"Die Hand will ich Dir…" The two girls each choose a girl from the circle, meaning there are two pairs in the inner circle. They hop, swinging their arms forwards and backwards in opposite directions of the moving circle using a simple skip step.
9	bow	"Mädel an der einen Hand…" The pairs and the circle stop. The circle holds hands. Every pair in the inner circle holds hands. To "Mädel an der einen" both steps sideways to the left, lift their arms straight up to shoulder height. To "einen" slightly tiptoe, to "hand" lower back down. To "Korb an der anderen": repeat same movements walking sideways to the right.
10 – 13	step over	
14 – 15		
16 -- 17	walking	To "So wollen…." both girls standing opposite each other, bow slightly, still holding hands.

| | | "Mädel an der anderen" as above (5 – 8)

"So setz ich mir…" indicate movement, using both hands

"Und mache mich …."", both girls belonging together, and the other pairs walk into the opposite direction to the outer circle. |
| --- | --- | --- |

This is where the song play starts anew. First there will be 4 pairs, later 8, in the end 16 pairs in the inner circle. This continues until the outer circle has completely dissolved.

Nasses Gras

Source: „So zum Tanze führ ich dich" by Otto Schmidt

Nasses Gras

Quellenangabe: „So zum Tanze führt ich dich", herausgegeben von Otto Schmidt.

1. Nas=ses Gras, nas=ses Gras auf der grü=nen Wie=se, hab ver=lo=ren mei=nen Schatz, werd ihn su=chen müf=fen, such ihn hier, such ihn da, un=ter die=sen al=len {wird gewiß wohl ei=ne sein, die mir wird ge=fal=len.} / {die=se in dem ro=ten Rock kann mir wohl ge=fal=len.} Dreh dich um, ich kenn dich nicht, bift du's o=der bift du's nicht, {nein, nein du bift es nicht, scher dich fort ich mag dich nicht.} / {ja, ja du bift es wohl, die ein Tänz=chen ha=ben foll.} Dort auf je=nem Ber=ge, fim=fe=rim=fim=fim, da tan=zen fie=ben Zwer=ge, fim=fe=rim=fim=fim, hei, dort auf je=nem Ber=ge, fim=fe=rim=fim=fim, da tan=zen fie=ben Zwerge, fim=fe=rim=fim=fim.

213

Pace	Form	Movement
1 – 8	circle	"Nasses Gras…" A large circle moves to the left. In the inner circle some of the girls walk behind each other into the opposite direction without holding hands.
9 – 12		
13 – 16	choose	"Such ihn hier…" The girls in the inner circle play the wording using hand movements.
17 – 20	turn	"Wird gewiß wohl eine sein…" The girls playing select a girl form the outer circle. To "gefallen", both circles stop, the girls from the inner circle stop in front of the girl from the outer circle they have chosen.
21 – 24	defence	
1 – 12	circle	"Dreh dich um…." One girl from the inner circle indicates a turn using hand movements, the chosen girl from the outer circle turns around herself.
13 – 20	choosing and turning	"Nein, nein…" The first girl makes a defending movement, the girl from the outer circle turns away.
21 – 24	hold hands	
25 -- 40	whirl	Both circles turn as above.

As above |

		"Ja, ja, Du bist es wohl...." The chosen girl will be grabbed by the hands and pulled into the circle. "Dort auf jenem Berge". The pairs whirl with outstretched arms around each other. The outer circle claps their hands in tune with the music. When repeating, just change the direction. A slight bow is to be done at the end. The dance now starts anew, with the chosen girls in the inner circle.

Es regnet auf der Brücke

Source: „So zum Tanze führ ich dich" by Otto Schmidt

Es regnet auf der Brücke

Quellenangabe: „So zum Tanze führ ich dich", herausgegeben von Otto Schmidt.

1. Es regnet auf der Brücke und ich werd naß.
Ich hab etwas verloren und weiß nicht was.

Schöne Jungfer, hübsch und fein, komm zu mir zum Tanz herein,

komm wir wollen tanzen und fröhlich sein.

2. Das Mädel mag nicht tanzen und fröhlich sein. So bin ich armer Bursche so ganz allein. Schöne Jungfer . . .

3. Ich ging einmal spazieren im grünen Wald und rief: „Herzallerliebste, ach komm doch bald!" Seht, das Mädel hübsch und fein kam zu mir zum Tanz herein, wollte mit mir tanzen und fröhlich sein.

Form an inner and an out circle, which move into opposite directions.

Pace	Form	Movement
1 – 4 repeat	Circle	Movement as above
5 – 6		"Schöne Jungfer hübsch und fein….". The girls from the inner circle select a beautiful maiden from the outer circle. Off you go.
7 --8	Inner circle in pairs	"Komm zu mir….", the girls of the inner circle extend their right hand to the girls of their outer circle and continue walking. The ones of the outer circle left over stand still.

Pace	Form	Movement
9 – 12 repeat	Whirl	"Komm wir wollen…" the pairs whirl to the right, they are holding hands and whirl in little steps around each other. The arms are almost stretched out, the feet close by another, so that despite the quick whirling, everything looks calm. The outer circle claps to
	2. Verse	the tune of the music.
1 – 4 repeat	Circle	
5 – 12		"Das Mädel mag nicht…." The girl from the outer circle walks away from the girl of the inner circle and returns to her outer circle. This circle keeps moving in its old direction. The inner
	3. Verse	circle in the opposite direction.
1 – 4 repeat	Circle	"Schöne Jungfer….". The girls of the inner circle keep trying to get the outer circle to dance to no avail.
5 – 12	Whirl	
5 – 12	Whirl	"Ich ging einmal…." The inner circle walks with crossed arms.
repat		"Seht die Jungfer…." The pairs who whirled together to the first verse, find each other as quickly as possible and whirl again. When performing in big circles it is often not that easy to

		find each other again. Do not run wild! The outer circle stands still and claps in tune with the music. "Seht die Jungfer….". When repeating whirl into the opposite direction.

Widewidewitt, min Mann is komen

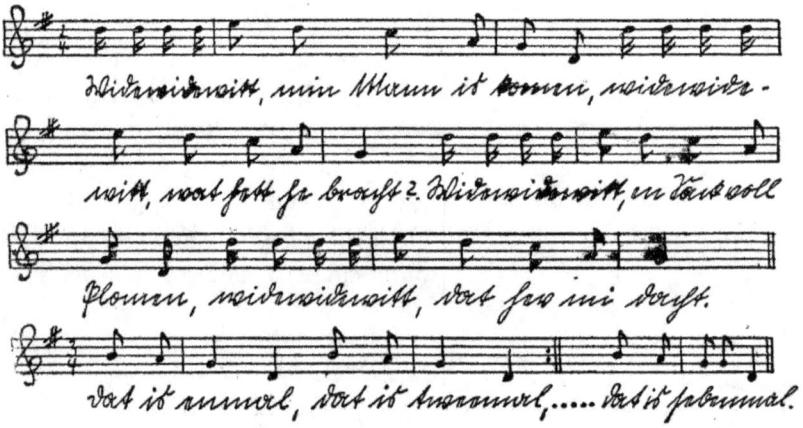

Widewidewitt, min Mann is komen (mein Mann ist gekommen)
Widewidewitt, wat hett he bracht? (Was hat er mitgebracht?)
Widewidewitt, en Sack voll Plomen (einen Sack voll Pflaumen)
Widewidewitt, dat hew mi dacht, (das habe ich mir gedacht)
Dat is enmal
Dat is tweemal
Dat is dreemal
Dat is veermal
Dat is fifmal
Dat is **sößmal**
Dat is sebenmal (das ist siebenmal

5. Widewidewitt, min Mann is komen

Description:

1. Pace 1 -- 4 All girls form a large circle and move in skip step to the right.

   Pace 5 – 8 Everybody moves to the right using skip step.

   Pace 9 all put the right foot forward upon "enmal".

2. Repeat the first part, pace 1 – 8, then pace 9 "dat is enmal" is extended to "dat is tweemal", this time it is the left foot, that moves forward.

3. Repeat of pace 1 --- 8, "dat is enmal, dat is tweemal," add "dat is dreemal", this is when the right knee is touching the floor.
The whole game repeats itself six times, each time extended by one like this:

dat is enmal – right foot forward
dat is tweemal – left foot forwards
dat is dreemal – right knee to the floor
dat is veermal – left knee to the floor
dat is fifmal – right elbow to the floor
dat is sößmal – left elbow to the floor
dat is sebenmal – touch the floor with your chin

Der Spielmann

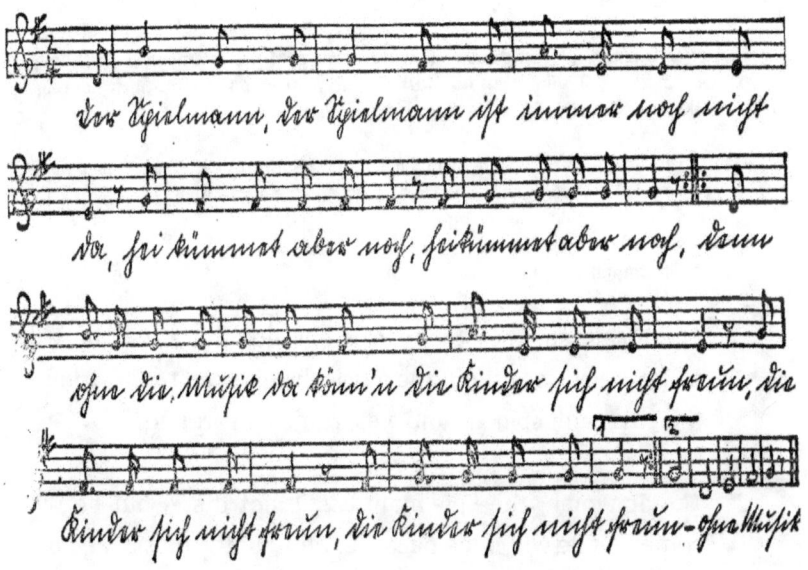

Der Spielmann, der Spielmann ist immer noch nicht da,
hei kümmt aber noch, hei kümmet aber noch,
denn ohen die Musik da könn'n die Kinder sich ich freun,
die Kinder sich nich freun, die Kinder sich nicht freun – ohne Musik

The musician, the musician, has still not come yet,
But he'll come, he'll come,
Because without the music, the children won't be happy,
The children won't be happy – without music.

2. Der Spielmann, der Spielmann ift immer no..) nicht da, hei kümmet aber noch, denn ohne die Mufike könn die Mädel ſich nicht drehn, die Mädel ſich nicht drehn, die Mädel ſich nicht drehn, ja ſich nicht drehn.

3. Der Spielmann, der Spielmann ift immer noch nicht da, hei kümmet aber noch, denn ohne die Mufike könn die Burſchen ſich nicht drehn, die Burſchen ſich nicht drehn, die Burſchen ſich nicht drehn, ja ſich nicht drehn.

4. Der Spielmann, der Spielmann ift immer noch nicht da, hei kümmet aber noch, denn ohne die Mufike kann die Hochzeit ja nicht ſein, die Hochzeit ja nicht ſein, die Hochzeit ja nicht ſein, ja nicht ſein.

6. Der Spielmann ift immer noch nicht da.

2. The Spielman, the Spielman is still not there, but he will come, because without the music the girls can't spin around, the girls can't spin around, yes, can't spin around

3. The Spielman, the Spielman, is still not there, but he will come, but he will come because, Without the music the boys can't spin around, the boys can't spin around, the boys can't Spin around – yes can't spin around

4. The Spielman, the Spielman is still not there, but he will come, but he will come, because without the music the marriage can't be, the marriage can't be, the marriage can't be. Yes, can't be.

5. The Spielman still hasn't arrived.

Description

1. Turn

Pace 1 – 2:   Alternately put forward the right, and then the left leg.

Pace 3 – 4:   The pairs tap each other on the shoulder.

Pace 5 – 12:   Every one hops in circles, first to the right and then left.

2. Turn

Pace 1 – 4:   Same as the first turn.

Pace 5 – 12:   The girls skip left and right around the boys. The boys clap their hands.

3. Turn

Pace 1 – 4:   Same as the first turn.

Pace 5 – 12:   same as 2. turn, but now it's the boys that are turning.

4. Turn

Pace 1 – 4:   Same as first turn.

Pace 5 – 12:   The pairs take up dancing position and dance a polka in direction of the circle turning.

5. Charade

Charade or the guessing game is an old parlor game. The guessing game is especially suitable for us, because it is a light form of an impromptu games and thus easily awakens fun. It addresses the spectator and involves them in the happenings, for they all must guess what the puzzle pictures may mean.

We can use a word as a puzzle by dividing it into single words, syllables or letters.

Once all single letters, syllables or words have been turned into a picture, the whole word is presented at the end.

For this game we will use words from the adventure world of the Jungmädel, like home afternoon, Jungmädel leader, field trip, parents evening etc. The meaning of the whole word must only be shown in the last picture, whereas the previous pictures depicting letters or syllables do not necessarily have to have anything to do with the meaning of the word. But we must adhere to the following:

1. The Jungmädel still feels a natural, unbiased joy in playing. Thus, training mimics or a large number of backdrops would be wrong and would destroy the natural and lively urge to play of the Jungmädel, which is to be preserved.

2. The JM leader allows the Jungmädel to make suggestions herself. The Jungmädel group will decide together which guessing games shall be

played and who takes up what role. This will bring fun and joy to the whole community.

3. You must inform the spectators, if the word is being presented in single letters, syllables or words and that one may have to add up the individual meanings to get to the meaning of the whole word at the end.

6. Home performances

The home game forms part of the Jungmädel service, just as any other song play or even song. It shall have educational value and is not just there to have fun. Values like presence of mind, observation, skilfulness etc. shall be strengthened using home games. – Each leader selects the home games that they fulfil these requirements. Home games without any purpose are not suitable for the Jungmädel service.

Examples:

1. Animal concert
One player is a lion, the second a sheep, the third a clock, the fourth a cat, etc.
One of them calls her comrade "Donkey" and that one answers with "eeeoooh", and then immediately call the ox, who will answer with "mooh" and thus, the game sparks on until someone calls out a name of an animal that is not present or gives the wrong answer. Every time someone makes a mistake; they have to deposit an item.

2. Everything with feathers flies high

Everyone sits round a table or stands in a circle. One calls out, and the one who have the names of the animals or objects that can fly raise their hands high in the air. For example:

"Everything with feathers flies high,
ducks fly, pigeons fly, bricks fly!"

However, when a girl raises her hand when the word bricks is mentioned, she needs to deposit an item!

3. Fishing game

All Jungmädel form a circle, standing closely together, hands pointing towards the middle. One girl in the middle is the fisher and recites the following:

I have been fishing
I have been fishing
I have been fishing the whole night
and never caught a fish!

During the reciting of the verse, she moves her hands over the stretched-out hands of the others, without touching them. Because she speaks the last sentence either very fast or very slow, no one knows when the verse is finished. She will try and tap one of the hands on the last syllable, meaning she will try and catch a fish. If she succeeds, the new girl will take her place as the fisher.

4. Searching for an object

All girls form a tight circle and one girl is in the middle. Shoulder is next to shoulder. Hands behind the back. An object is passed from one to the other and the girl in the middle must guess where the object is. The girl is touched and teased with the object every now and then, before being passed on quickly. If the girl finds the object, she swaps places with the girl with whom the object was found.

5. Word order

We are adding words together. Sitting in a circle one throws a knotted scarf to another and at the same time says a noun like "window". The Jungmädel who caught the scarf quickly answers with a second noun like "glass" or "pane", both words are then put together making "window glass" or "window pane".

The second girl then throws the scarf to a third girl, using the last noun used "glass" and the third girl quickly answers her saying "pearl". And so, it continues, until one runs out words or uses a wrong one, in which case she has to leave and object as a deposit.

6. Guess the tradesman

One girl mimics the movements of a tradesman, the other will have to guess which trade is being displayed.

7. Guess the song

There are different ways of doing this, you can clap the rhythm with your hands, and one Jungmädel, previously send outside now has to guess the song, or you can give a word to each Jungmädel. One then asks a series of questions and the Jungmädel inserts her word into the answer. Detecting the correct words should then give the beginning or the title of a song.

8. Guess the town

All sit in a circle. One Jungmädel describes a town without mentioning its name using descriptions of tourist attractions, buildings, rivers nearby etc. Whoever guesses correctly may give a description of the next town. (You can do the same with mountain ranges, German landscapes etc.)

9. Relays using home games

These are especially good to play if there is a large crowd of Jungmädel, who will be divided into groups (at the most ten per group). They sit in circles or around tables. All circles will now receive the same task, which must be solved in a competition.

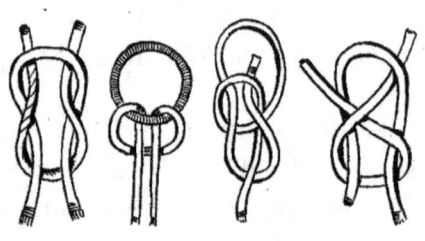

1. Every Jungmädel must tie a knot into a rope, that is being passed around. The knots must all be tied at the same distance from each other. Which circle finishes first?

2. Untie the knots

3. The first Jungmädel in the circle holds one lite and unlit flashlight. She lights the second and extinguishes the first. She passes each flash light to the next girl. The second Jungmädel continues. Which circle finishes first? You may find that some will extinguish both lights in sheer excitement.

4. A box of matches is passed from nose to nose. There are endless possibilities and plenty of tasks with which the Jungmädel leader can show her ideas.

10. Release the deposit

This game is designed as a punishment for those who have been inattentive and had to leave a deposit in the first place. No one may refuse to release their deposit.

Everyone will have to tolerate a little tease in good humour, as long as those, who determine the punishment are not too harsh. Everything dangerous or painful shall be eliminated and even during the greatest of fun everyone should know the limits.

The following ways to play this are recommended:

Sit down on the floor and stand back up without the use of hands.
Using your hand throw a shadow game onto a wall.
Make animal voices.
Tell a story in which all the names of all fellow players appear.
Hold a penalty speech.
Tell a tale of lies.

11. Fast speaking sentences:

Fischers Fritze fischt frische Fische, frische Fische fischt Fischers Fritze.
Metzger wetz dein Messer, dann schneidets noch viel besser.
Große Krebse krabbeln in dem Korbe.

12. Quizzes

It huffs and puffs along the street
but it has no lung
it eats the snow like butter
but it has no tongue.
Answer: A thawing wind.

If you want me to give you plenty
you have to bury me first.
Answer: The seed.

In spring I bring you joy
in summer I cool you down
in winter I keep you warm.
Answer: The tree.

Goes round and round the tree
but doesn't go in.
Answer: The bark.

The poor thing
it has a crown but no head
and also
one foot and no shoe.
Answer: The mushroom

7. Story telling

Story telling has a very special place in the work with the Jungmädel. The most beautiful fairy and folk tales from the old times of our nation are being told. The art of  storytelling has vanished more and more over the last centuries. Only very few people are still able to tell a story. But it is not really an "art". All we must do is to be capable again to tell stories freely and lively.

When conducting a home afternoon, it is impossible for the leader to read through the home afternoon folder from beginning to end. The Jungmädel would soon get bored and lose their attention. Because they shall experience what they are being told during a home afternoon, the Jungmädel leader must be able to hold her talks freely. But that does not mean she should learn by heart. The leader should read through the pages a few times until she is familiar with the contents then speak about the matter without clutching to words.

The Jungmädel themselves will approach story telling naturally, for they do not yet know any fear, but are able to speak and talk freely.

The home afternoon and the parents evening are not possible without story telling at all. But what do we talk about?

1. Fairy tales 2. Folk tales from the region 3. German heroic legends
4. Funny tales and anecdotes   5. Experiences during the JM service.

1. The collection of fairy tales we use for the Jungmädel service is that of the brothers Grimm with drawings from Otto Ubbelohde. In addition, we can use the German book of fairy tales from (Eugene) Diederichs (publisher), Jena.

2. Folk tales from the region will be gathered together by the Jungmädel themselves. They will have already heard a lot of tales from parents and grandparents about their local region, or even learned them in school. Those regional folk tales will be collated beautifully written in an exercise book.

3. We will read the German heroic legends from the books of Leopold Weber and Gustav Schultz. In addition to this, we will use the folder of the Reichs youth leadership about and learn about Gudrun.

4. Funny tales and anecdotes for us are the pranks of Eulenspiegel, Rübezahl, Münchhausen, the seven Swabians, and the Schildbürger.

We must not speak about everything a poet formed and wrote, for our language is not as good as his and will never be as accomplished as that of a poet. Thus, we will stick to the material mentioned here. We use poetry much less than story telling in our Jungmädel work.

8. Arts and crafts in the First Year
a) Work in Summer
During the six months of summer, arts and crafts are on pause with the ten-year-old. They will mainly be concentrating on sports and games. We will only craft small practical items for field trips, camps and our service during this time.

Sewing of little wash bags with rubber backing for our trips,

a skipping rope,

a ball,

a folder made from cardboard for trip reports

how to fold a beaker

whistles made from willow

and platting using rushes

The first task every Jungmädel has is to make a skipping rope and a ball for sports. The rope will be twisted from twine or crochet using fingers. Two wooden parcel grips will be used to make the grips.

The ball should have the size and the weight of a batting ball. It will be made from an old rubber bicycle tire filled with corks.

b) Work in Winter
Winter work up until Christmas will be governed with the Winterhilfswerk (WHW) in mind. The Jungmädel must be made aware that the national community has requirements they are already able to meet and that they can contribute to the community with their work. December is governed by Christmas. We will make simple decorative articles from paper, like gluing lanterns or transparent pictures (fairy tale pictures). We will also bind our own advent wreath. In addition, we will specially make table decorations.

For the Winterhilfswerk and as Christmas presents:

Building kits and building bricks

Stick-in figures for sand

Spinning tops made from twine reels or parcel grips

Jumping Jacks

Flower sticks

Folded boxes from cardboard

Wall calendars

Counting and puzzle games

Folder from coloured cardboard for song sheets

Drawing and painting

Sculptures

Christmas decorations

Lanterns

Lightboxes

Making a wreath from fir branches

Table decorations for the JM or parents' home

Candle holders

Animals and little figures, made from nuts, dried plums, apples and figs

Folded doilies

c) Examples
1. Stick-in figures for sand

Material:	6mm ply
	paint or stain, possibly varnish
Tools:	Hack saw
	File
	Sand paper

First of all, we will spare a though of what figures we want to create for our sand stick game. You will find a multitude of possibilities. We can make figures for:

a farm or
a mill
a fairy tale
a community of dwarfs
a zoological garden etc.

First of all be draw our figures on a piece of paper and then transfer them to tracing paper. Do not draw figures with lots of detail and edges, these will break all to easily. Always try and draw keeping the outlines a simple as possible.

Now file the edges smooth at a right angle and paint the figures with colourful with poster colours, opaque colours or using stain.
Once the paint is dry add a finishing layer of varnish or rub the figures with floor wax.

2. Building bricks in a bag

Material:	Building bricks
	water soluble stain
Tools:	File
	Sandpaper

A building set is a toy that will lead to new pleasures each time and thus brings joy to every child.

Go the carpenter's workshop and get yourself some wood offcuts, as different as possible. If they are a bit too large, take a saw and cut them to the desired size. You can also add a few basic bricks cut of a batten.

You must now carefully smooth the blocks with the file and afterwards first with rough and then with smooth sandpaper.

Next you can paint the blocks with varnish or water stain. Once they are completely dry they will need to be rubbed off with floor wax.

Once we have made a number of different colour blocks, we will sew a little cloth bag with a colourful drawstring to store them in.

3. Straw coaster

Using the best straws we make small plat, with three, four or more straws. Every time when one straw comes to the end, work in a new one. Any objectionable spike or this bits will be cut off with scissors. A thick dawning needle or upholstery needle will be threaded with some thin twine and the straw plat will be wound up and stitched together, with the thread as invisible as possible. You can use different shapes, rounds, squares, to and fro. You can even make larger mats by stiching different parts together or even on top of each other. We can use them as floor mats, or behind a bench to keep the warmth in or to rest something on.

4. Balls

Material:	Old wine bottle corks
	Wood wool
	left over wool

| Tools: | Knife |
| | Scissors and needle |

We cut two wine corks lengthwise apart, place them together with the round backs against each other and string them tightly together. Then we wrap the corks tightly with wood wool and afterwards wrap wool around the ball very tightly.

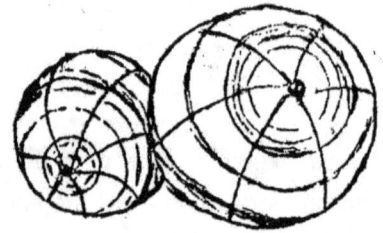

Once the ball is completely round, with a diameter of around 20 cm, we start covering the ball. The ball is covered with a tension thread that crosses on the two opposite poles. It should be an uneven number of threads.

Now you take a colourful yarn and thread it around the ball, picking up one of the tension threads and leaving the next. Almost like a weave. Pick up nice colours for your ball and distribute the yarn evenly around.

If you are making more than one ball, then you can also make a ball net, that you can crochet using the chain mesh technique.

5. Spinning tops made from yarn reels

Material: yarn reels
parcel grips
poster colors
clear varnish

Tools: Hack saw or fine saw
Round file

Cut the yarn reel in half according to the drawing below, using a thick hack saw blade or a fine saw. Using the round file, extend the hole, so that it fits the wooden parcel grip.

You can then decorate the spinning tops using the poster colours in a fun way. Once the paint is dry apply a coat of clear varnish to make them shine or rub floor wax all over.

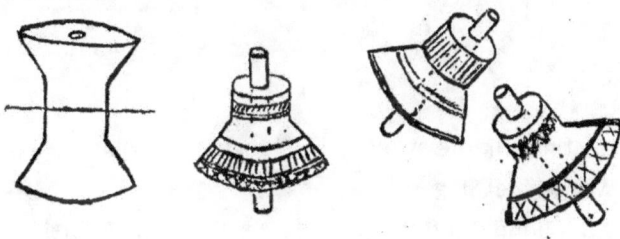

Reference to available service regulations and specialist books

Apart from the training guideline in front of you, the following training guidelines and specialist books are to be used for the educational service of the first year when dealing with the relevant subjects:

a) Service instructions:

Dv. JM 1 „Dienstordnung für den Jungmädelbund"
(Service instruction for the JM)
Dv. JM 7 „Gesundheitsordnung der HJ
(Health instruction of the HJ)
Dv. JM 8 „ Lagerordnung der HJ "
(Camp instructions of the HJ)
Av. JM 10 " Der Gesundheitsdienst" *(The health service)*

b) Specialist books

Leaflets for conducting a home evening: Die Jungmädelschaft
Our Song book: Wir Mädel Singen
The magazine of the Bund Deutscher Mädel: Das Deutsche Mädel

Books for games: Mädelspiele
(Games for girls)
(Publisher: Vogelreiter Verlag, 1.80 Reichsmark)

Spielvolk
(Games for folk)
(Publisher: Hirth Verlag, Breslau, 0.40 Reichsmark)

Additional Books

"Through Innocent Eyes – The Chosen Girls of the Hitler Youth"
Author: Cynthia A. Sandor
Publisher: BDM History Publishing
ISBN# 978-0999755006

Girls in Service
The Official Handbook of the Bund Deutscher Mädel
Publisher: BDM History Publishing
ISBN# 978-0999755075

BDM History Collection – The Young Girls Achievement Badge
Publisher: BDM History Publishing
ISBN# 978-0999755044

Reflections – The Story of Dorothy Swanson
Wife of an 82nd Airborne Paratrooper
ISBN# 978-0999755020

"In Den Bann Gezogen"
Author: Cynthia A. Sandor
ISBN# 979-8985456714

All books can be purchased directly from the publisher at:
https://bdmhistory.com

ABOUT THE BOOK COVER

This illustration is the work of Terry Breycha-Scholz (sometimes spelled Breyche-Scholz), a German illustrator known for her charming depictions of children. The style is characteristic of mid-20th century European children's book illustrations and postcards.

Information on the Artwork and Artist:

Artist: Terry Breycha-Scholz was a German illustrator who created numerous heartwarming scenes of children in rural settings, often used for postcards and book illustrations.

Style: Her work often features a delicate watercolor and ink style, capturing a nostalgic and innocent view of childhood, similar in theme to other popular German and Swedish illustrators of the era like Fritz Baumgarten and Jenny Nyström.

Theme: The image depicts three children in traditional German or Austrian attire (lederhosen and dirndl-style clothing) in a rustic village setting, seemingly on an errand or outing with a basket and a small wooden cart of baked goods. The presence of the signature and the style suggests it was likely produced as a print or postcard.

Period: Her work was popular around the 1930s to 1950s

ADDITIONAL NOTES

ADDITIONAL NOTES